HUDDERSFIELD'S
NINETEENTH-CENTURY
YORKSHIRE XI

HUDDERSFIELD'S NINETEENTH-CENTURY YORKSHIRE XI

J.R. Ellam

ATHENA PRESS
LONDON

HUDDERSFIELD'S NINETEENTH-CENTURY
YORKSHIRE XI
Copyright © J.R. Ellam 2004

All Rights Reserved

ISBN 1 84401 302 2

First Published 2004 by
ATHENA PRESS
Queen's House, 2 Holly Road
Twickenham TW1 4EG
United Kingdom

Printed for Athena Press

Foreword

This group of men have long since departed and are just a faded memory in long-forgotten scorecards, and their achievements are only remembered in obscure quizzes or taproom argument. But they all played a part in shaping local, county, and international cricket, and while I was doing the research I changed my views about the first Ashes match; and this is my way of keeping their achievements alive for a little bit longer.

Introduction

I have picked eleven cricketers who were born in and around the Huddersfield area, and started playing cricket for Yorkshire before the turn of the twentieth century. Some even played in Yorkshire representative XIs before the formation of the Yorkshire County Cricket Club, at the Adelphi Hotel, Sheffield, on January 8th 1863; the subscription was no less than 10s 6d (52.5p) (a weaver would earn about 21s (£1.05) a week).

Player	Career
J. Berry	1849-1867
L. Greenwood	1861-1875
J. Thewlis	1861-1875
E. Lockwood	1868-1888
A. Greenwood	1869-1880
A. Hill	1871-1883
E. Lumb	1872-1886
W. Bates	1877-1887
G.H. Hirst	1889-1921
S. Haigh	1895-1913
W. Rhodes	1898-1930

In my opinion they would have given any cricketing XI a good run for their money, and that includes international XIs. This might seem a bit boastful, but when you see some of their achievements it doesn't seem too unlikely. They include:

- The first player from this region to play in a Yorkshire XI
- The first Yorkshire player to score a century in a county match
- The first Yorkshire player to score a double century in a county match

- The first bowler to take a wicket in a Test match
- The first player to take a catch in a Test match
- The first English bowler to take a hat-trick in a Test match
- The first player to score 50+ runs in an innings and take 10+ wickets in a Test match
- The only player to take 200+ wickets and score 2,000+ runs in a season.

When you break the XI down it is comprised of two former Yorkshire captains, L. Greenwood and E. Lockwood: they are joined by the strong batting line-up of J. Berry, J. Thewlis, E. Lumb and A. Greenwood, leaving the difficult decision of who would open the innings. At first look the bowling line-up seems a bit weak, with just S. Haigh and A. Hill; but they are backed up by the formidable all-round abilities of W. Bates, G.H. Hirst and W. Rhodes; also most of the other players have taken wickets in county matches. I know that the purist will have noticed that there is no wicketkeeper in the XI, but both E. Lockwood and J. Thewlis have spent some time behind the timbers (Lockwood taking 2 stumpings and Thewlis 1 stumping).

I could have made the research a lot easier by just looking at the 'Who's Who' of the Lascelles Hall cricket club, because they had twenty players who went on to play for Yorkshire in the period I was looking at. Though I have tried to pick players from the other cricket clubs, I still have had to include six players from the Lascelles Hall club, just like Yorkshire did when they played against Derbyshire at Derby on August 20th 1877, and all bar two were born in the Kirkheaton Parish.

The research was also made harder because most of them and their achievements have long since been forgotten, so I had to do most of the research by reading through the local papers (the *Huddersfield Daily Examiner* and the *Huddersfield Weekly Examiner*). The early results and reports are a bit sketchy, but they pointed me in the direction of a series of articles by 'Old Ebor' written in the *Yorkshire Evening Post* and printed towards the end of the nineteenth century.

I have tried to gauge how their achievements were reported at the time, I have also picked some snippets out of the papers about their careers and lives; one of them even managed to get one over W.G. Grace! I also came across a secret about one of the players that his family has managed to keep quiet for over a century.

I have also tried to find out what happened to them after their careers were over. This was made harder by some of the players just going into obscurity; but for some, tragedy and misfortune just seemed to follow them. One of them went on to umpire what is now known as the first match in the Ashes series (in my opinion if they had picked Lockwood there wouldn't have been an Ashes series).

John Berry

John Berry was born on January 10th 1823 at Dalton, and baptised on May 12th 1823. He was the eldest child of Joseph and Amelia Berry (née Austen), who were married at Kirkheaton Parish Church on October 31st 1822. He had four brothers: George and Benjamin (twins), born in 1829; Ephraim, born in 1832; and James, born in 1834. There were five sisters: Ann, born in 1824; Eliza, born in 1826; Martha, born in 1838; Mary, born in 1840; and Isabella, born in 1843. The last son, James, only lived for nine months.

They grew up at Long Lane Bottom, Dalton, and they followed their father into the hand-loom weaving trade. John spent his spare time in the summer playing cricket for both the early local cricket clubs, Lascelles Hall and Dalton.

Berry would often miss Sunday school to practise his cricket in a near-by wood, and if the authorities had found out he would have had a hefty fine to pay, because it was an offence to work on the Sabbath, let alone play sport. When he was in his early twenties, Berry would have incurred even more of their wrath if they had found out he had played in a one-man match on a Sunday, for a reputed £25.

In 1847, Berry was asked along with his Uncle George to play in two matches for a team made up of players from Bradford and Dalton, against Sheffield, for £44 each match. (Note that men's Wellingtons then cost 19s (95p) to 21s (£1.05); tobacco cost 3s 3d (16p) per lb.; and a schoolmaster was on £20 to £35 per annum plus house.) The first match was at the Hyde Park ground in Sheffield, on June 28th 1847, and Sheffield won easily by an innings. The second match was at the Horton Lane ground, Bradford, on July 12th. Sheffield won again, but the game didn't end without a bit of controversy. It was when George Berry was given out in a similar way to the one that W.G. Grace used in the 1882 Test, and John Berry was given out when he walked off the field in disgust.

John and George Berry were at the wickets, and the later had obtained 7, but in running the last run, his hat fell off, and before the ball had finally settled in the hands of the wicket keeper, G. Berry walked out of his crease to put on his hat, and the wicket was very properly put down. The umpire (the one for Bradford and Dalton) was appealed to, and he gave the man out, upon which John Berry became so enraged that he refused to bat any more; consequently, his wicket was lost to the party.

Sheffield & Rotherham Independent
July 17th 1847

Berry married Harriet Thewlis, who was the sister of John Thewlis, at Kirkheaton Parish Church on September 21st 1848.

Most of Berry's cricketing activities went unreported, and not being able to get access to the early records I cannot be sure about most of his career. I do know he was picked to play for a Yorkshire XI against Kent at Hyde Park, Sheffield, on May 20th 1849. He only scored 10 runs in the first innings and got a duck in the second innings. He was struggling with his form, and against Sheffield at the Victory Ground, Woodhouse Moor, Leeds, on July 9th 1849, he got a duck in the first innings and 7 runs in the second.

Berry started to turn his form round, and against Lancashire at Hyde Park, Sheffield, on July 16th 1849, he scored 3 runs in the first innings, but his 23 not out in the second helped steer Yorkshire to victory. In Yorkshire's return match against Sheffield at Hyde Park, Sheffield, on August 6th, he scored 55 not out in the first innings, and he followed it up with 10 runs in the second.

Their first child, Finetta, was born on October 1st 1849. Everything was going well for the Berrys.

Berry was asked to be a professional for the Sheffield Wednesday cricket club in 1850. He was also picked for a Gentlemen against Player game at the York Cricket Ground, on September 23rd 1850, but he only scored 2 runs and 5 runs. Berry moved his family to Sheffield, where the Duke of Norfolk employed him as his gamekeeper, to help him make ends meet in the winter months. The Duke of Norfolk also asked Berry to teach his son the art of the game.

Berry was still playing for Dalton when he could, and in 1851 he was part of the Dalton side that challenged Sheffield – then the undisputed champions of Yorkshire – to a match for £100. (Devon butter was 78s (£3.90) to 84s (£4.20) per cwt or 8¼d (3½p) to 9d (4p) per lb.; Cheddar cheese was 56s (£2.80) to 68s (£3.40) per cwt or 6d (2½p) to 7¼d (3¼p) per lb.; Cheshire cheese was 52s (£2.10) to 70s (£3.50) per cwt or 5.5d (2¼p) to 7.5d (3¼p) per lb.) The match generated a lot of interest in the region and even the local paper got involved.

Our sporting readers will no doubt learn with pleasure, that a grand Cricket Match will be played at Manchester, on Monday, Tuesday, and Wednesday, next, between eleven of Dalton and eleven of Sheffield, for £100 a-side. Much excitement prevails as to the result of the match, the Sheffield players having for a long period, acted the Napoleons of Yorkshire in the cricket field, are rather ruffled to have their supremacy disputed; the Dalton club believe they will be enabled to prove themselves a Wellington as at Waterloo, upon this occasion; the betting is brisk – the call being in favour of Dalton.

Huddersfield Weekly Examiner
September 27th 1851

The match was played at a neutral ground in Manchester on July 29th 1851. Dalton scored 101 and 134 and Sheffield scored 102 and 127, which meant Dalton won the match by 7 runs. Berry only scored 25 runs (16 and 9) but he took 4 wickets (3 and 1) and he held on to 2 catches.

The Berrys had another three children while he was with Sheffield. Two sons were born, Tom in 1852 and Dick in 1859. A daughter, Alice, arrived in 1855.

At the end of the 1859 season Sheffield presented Berry with a silver cup for being the best player that season. Everything was going well for him, but sadly his wife, Harriet, died at the age of 38, in August 1860.

With Berry spending more of his time away from home travelling up and down the country playing cricket, his mother and father helped him out by looking after the children.

Berry was back in favour with Yorkshire, and he was picked to play in a match against the Hallam cricket club at Hyde Park,

Sheffield, on July 18th 1861, for £100. Here he scored another 50 runs in the first innings and then 10 runs. He was also picked by Yorkshire to play in both their matches against Surrey, and at the end of the first match at the Oval on May 23rd 1861, the Surrey committee gave the Yorkshire team £5 10s, which works out at 10 shillings (50p) each. (Men's shoes cost from 5s 5d (27½p) to 6s (30p); a cheap return by rail from Huddersfield to Scarborough was 7s (35p) and a return by rail from Huddersfield to the Chester races was 12s 6d (62½p) first class, and 6s 6d (32½p) second class.)

Berry spent as much time as he could with his children at his parents' house in Dalton, and while he was there he met Elizabeth Roebuck. They were married at Kirkheaton Parish Church on March 2nd 1862.

Berry was picked by Yorkshire in the 1862 season, and when Yorkshire played Kent at Brammall Lane on June 2nd, which was the first time they had played each other since 1849, Berry was the only player left from the 1849 match. Berry was struggling to find his form, but at the end of the season he was picked to play for a Yorkshire XIV against the All England XI, and he was the top scorer with 28 runs in the first innings and followed it up with 18 runs.

At the start of the 1863 season, Accrington cricket club were looking for a professional to boost their ranks. The members were split between Berry and another professional called Nicholson. Three of the members behind Berry went to see him at Sheffield and iron out an agreement with him. When they got back to Accrington they hurriedly arranged a meeting and they engaged Berry for 42s (£2.40) per week with a 3s (15p) win bonus. (A printer was on about 28s (£1.40); a policeman was on about 15s (75p) and a general labourer was on about 14s (70p) per week.) So Berry moved the family over the border to Lancashire, while his eldest daughter, Finetta, stopped in Dalton to help take care of her grandparents.

Berry was also picked to play in the first Yorkshire County side against Surrey at the Oval on June 4th 1863. He opened the innings for Yorkshire with his former brother-in-law, J. Thewlis. He had a decent match, scoring 35 in his only innings, and taking

4 wickets. He was a bit unlucky in Yorkshire's first home match, which was against Nottingham at Bradford on June 22nd.

> *Yorkshire sent in John Berry and John Thewlis, Jackson and Wootton bowling. The evening had become gloomy, an unpleasant drizzling rain was falling, and the light was fading, both conditions unfavourable to the batsmen. Jackson's third ball found its way to Berry's stumps, and he was forced to retire without having made a hit. This was discouraging for the Yorkshire players, as Berry is justly regarded as an excellent cricketer, and as done yeoman service both this and previous years on behalf of his county.*

Huddersfield Weekly Examiner
June 27th 1863

Berry didn't fare much better in Yorkshire's return match against Surrey at Brammall Lane, Sheffield, on July 27th, but Yorkshire still managed to prevail.

> *Berry, Thewlis, J. Stephenson and Waud were successively sent in at the commencement of the Yorkshire innings, and though among the best batsmen, they were all dismissed for an aggregate of nine runs. The chances were now so greatly against Yorkshire that 20 to 1 were bet on Surrey.*

Leeds Intelligencer
August 1st 1863

Yorkshire persisted with Berry, and when they played Surrey at Sheffield on June 13th 1864, he was awarded £2 for his performance. (Tea was then 2s 7d (13p) per lb.; a cheap return from Huddersfield to Scarborough by rail was 6s (30p).) Berry was struggling with his consistency and he was severely hurt in his first innings against Cambridgeshire at Brammall Lane, Sheffield, on July 25th; but he managed to bat in Yorkshire's second innings, and he was the top scorer with 39 runs. Berry then got the acclaim for his second innings performance in Yorkshire's last match of the season, which was against Kent on September 19th 1864; after only scoring 15 runs in the first innings he made amends with 41 not out in the second.

John Berry played admirably for his 41 (not out) and never gave a chance and we are glad to see that John Berry is playing so finely this season; he has on several occasions rendered excellent service to his county – long may he continue to do so.

Huddersfield Weekly Examiner
September 24th 1864

Berry was still active with Accrington and he was also still in touch with his old club, Dalton, and in 1865 they arranged to play each other twice. He had a poor start to the 1865 season for Yorkshire, and he was dropped after the second game. With some of Yorkshire's professionals refusing to play, they decided to bring Berry back for the last match. This was against Kent at Gravesend on August 24th, and in the first innings he scored 78 runs, which is his highest score for Yorkshire.

Some players were still refusing to play in the 1866 season, so Yorkshire decided to play the amateurs for their games. Everything was resolved for the 1867 season, and Berry was picked for one last match for Yorkshire on June 20th. It was against Lancashire at Whalley, and in his only innings Berry managed to get 27 runs. At the end of the season Berry decided to call it a day, and he retired from first class cricket in 1867.

BERRY'S CAREER FIGURES:

Batting
Runs   945
Average   16.01

Bowling
Wickets   12
Runs   149
Average   18.62

Others
Catches   12
County Championship
1867

Shortly after his retirement, his father, Joseph, died at the age of 70 in the December of 1867. Berry got a job in a weaving shed, and he was still an active member of the Accrington team, and he used all his professional guile to draw a match against East Lancashire. With East Lancashire only needing 9 runs to win and the time nearly up, Berry was bowling so he started picking at the spikes in his boots to make it look like there was something wrong with them. He subsequently ran the time out and the match was declared a draw.

Berry moved to the Enfield cricket club in 1869 and he stayed there until he finally gave up playing in 1872. After he stopped playing he didn't give up with the game fully. He was an umpire in the local leagues, and he would also give the young up-and-coming players his advice when they asked for it.

Berry was also an avid follower of brass band music, and he was particularly enthusiastic follower of the Accrington Old Band, and they honoured him by making him a trustee, which enabled him to get to see more of their performances. He outlived his sons, Tom dying in the December of 1879 and Dick dying in the December of 1885.

Berry kept himself active and he won a veterans' hundred yards race in 1890. His youngest daughter, Alice, married James Hindle in 1891. In 1892 he played for a veterans' side at the Huddersfield United ground, Marsh. He managed to put on 68 runs, but it isn't clear if he was still able to play his favourite stroke of hitting the ball under his left leg while he was standing on his right leg!

The veterans' match offered his mother, Amelia, her last chance of seeing her son play cricket, and not long after the match Amelia died at the age of 90 in the October of 1892. The death of Amelia enabled his eldest daughter, Finetta, to move to Accrington to be with the rest of the family.

John Berry died at the age of 72, just before noon on Tuesday, February 26th 1895; he was buried on the Saturday at the Accrington Cemetery. It seems that most of the town turned out to pay their last respects to 'Old John' and lined the streets to watch the cortège en route to the cemetery. Even the local MP, Mr. J.F. Leese QC, sent a large wreath to honour him. His passing is marked with a large headstone.

Luke Greenwood

Luke Greenwood was born on July 13th 1834 at Cowms, Lepton; he was the fourth child of Richard and Grace Greenwood (née Thornton). He had two brothers – Job Thornton, born in 1825 and John Thomas, born in 1832; and two sisters – Sarah, born in 1824, and Mary Hannah, born in 1843. They grew up in the Lascelles Hall area of Huddersfield and he went on to follow in the family tradition and became a hand-loom weaver. He started playing cricket at an early age with his brothers for the Lascelles Hall club.

In 1850, Luke's father, Richard, died at the age of 48, when Luke was only 15 years of age. His mother, Grace, died just five years later at the age of 51, and the running of the house was left to his elder sister, Sarah.

In 1858, Greenwood saw an advert in a paper for a cricketer placed by the Duke of Sutherland. He applied for the post and to his surprise he was successful and he was offered it, and he duly accepted. He stopped with the Duke until he got an offer in 1861 from Lord Lichfield, and he played his first big game against Parr's All England XI. He took 5 wickets for 30 runs. After the match, Parr poached Greenwood for the Broughton club of Manchester, and he was invited to play in the first North against South match at his new ground.

As far as I can tell, Greenwood's first appearance for a Yorkshire XI was against Hallam at Hyde Park, Sheffield, on July 18th 1861, in a match for £100. (Bordeaux was then 14s (70p) per dozen bottles and port was 18s (90p) per dozen bottles.) He scored 25 runs and 63 runs to help Yorkshire win the match. Greenwood was also picked for Yorkshire against Surrey at Brammall Lane, Sheffield, on July 22nd 1861, but he got a duck and 14 runs. Despite this, Yorkshire still managed to win the game.

With Greenwood now playing in more Yorkshire and England representative sides, he decided to concentrate most of his time to practice and playing the odd match for Lascelles Hall. But all through his career he was hired in the spring as a coach by several clubs all over the country – Winchester, Rugby, Stoneyhurst, and Dublin University, just to name a few. It was while he was at Stoneyhurst that he recommended Allen Hill to them.

Greenwood was taken ill at the end of the 1862 season, and Yorkshire overlooked him for the 1863 season (which was the first official season after their formation in the January of that year).

Greenwood came back in the 1864 season and he managed to get his name back on the Yorkshire team sheet. He was playing well, and against Surrey at Sheffield on June 13th he scored 65 and 10, and took 3 wickets in the first innings, and after the match he was presented with £5 for his excellent play. (Tea was 2s 7d (13p) per lb.; a cheap return from Huddersfield to Harrogate by rail was 4s (20p), and a cheap return from Huddersfield to Scarborough by rail was 6s (30p).)

He followed it up by scoring 4 runs and 59 runs against Cambridgeshire at Parker's Piece on July 4th 1864. In the return match at Brammall Lane, Sheffield, on July 25th he only scored 12 runs and 14 runs, but he took 9 wickets for 44 runs (4-22 and 5-22); and in the first innings he was bowled for 16 consecutive overs, which only cost him 5 runs. This effort took its toll on Greenwood and he was taken ill just before the return match against Surrey at the Oval on August 1st, and it forced him to miss the rest of the season.

This time local cricketers arranged a benefit match to help Greenwood through the winter. It was between eleven Huddersfield Players against seventeen Gentlemen of Huddersfield, and Greenwood. It was played at Lockwood on October 7th and it raised £17.

Greenwood was picked for the United England XI at Lord's on June 4th 1865 and took 5 wickets (2 and 3), but he only scored 3 and 8. He fared better with the bat for Yorkshire against Surrey at Brammall Lane, Sheffield, on June 19th, scoring 83 runs and 10 runs. This got him picked for his first appearance for the Players against the Gentlemen at the Oval on July 3rd. However, he was bowled for 5 runs in the first innings by a player making his debut for the Gentlemen called W.G. Grace. He did a bit better in the second innings, scoring 31 runs.

He wasn't picked for the second Gentlemen v Players match at Lord's, but he was able to get to Trent Bridge in time to play for Yorkshire against Nottinghamshire on July 27th 1865. He took 9 wickets (7-43 and 2-?), and he scored 24 runs and 1 run, but Yorkshire still managed to lose the match.

In a double wedding with his sister at Kirkheaton on June 25th 1866, Greenwood married Amelia Jessop, and his sister, Mary Hannah, married a Lascelles Hall and Yorkshire team-mate, William Shotton. His only match for Yorkshire was just a month before their first child, Emma, was born on September 16th 1866.

Greenwood and G. Freeman bowled unchanged against Surrey at the Oval on June 6th 1867, bowling them out for 92 runs and 62 runs, with Greenwood taking 11 wickets for 71 runs (6 and 5). Greenwood stopped in London to play alongside W.G. Grace for the England XI against Middlesex on June 10th.

When he returned to the Yorkshire side, he and Freeman were asked to repeat the feat of bowling unchanged again. This time it was against Lancashire at Whalley, Manchester, on June 20th 1867. They bowled Lancashire out for 57 runs and 75 runs, with Greenwood taking 7 wickets (3 and 4) for 76 runs.

The first time Yorkshire played a county match in Dewsbury, which was at the Savile ground against Cambridgeshire on July 25th 1867, Greenwood took 8 wickets for 31 runs in the first innings, and his effort was rewarded as follows.

Greenwood made the best average in bowling, and he was presented with a rug.

Huddersfield Daily Examiner
July 25th 1867

Because of an injury he was only able to bowl a few overs in the second innings.

1868 started well for the Greenwoods; they had a second child, John Herbert, on April 11th 1868, and Luke was also busy playing cricket for Yorkshire and representative sides. But things soon started to go wrong for them; Luke was involved in a life-threatening accident, which got the following report:

The Manchester and Leeds daily papers of Thursday published a paragraph stating that an omnibus accident had occurred at a place in Nottinghamshire, by which Luke Greenwood was so seriously injured that he was not expected to recover. On making further inquiry, we were glad to find that this was an exaggeration of Greenwood's case, and that, although the injuries sustained by him are serious, they are not likely to prove fatal.

Sad, however, was the accident for Greenwood, than whom a more esteemed cricketer does not exist, was so seriously hurt that, had not Dr. Fielding been close at hand to apply proper remedies, his life would probably have been forfeited. As it is, he lies with dangerous internal injuries, which medical men say must confine him to bed for some six weeks.

Huddersfield Daily Examiner
August 8th 1868

While he was recovering from the accident, Greenwood was persuaded to take out a claim for compensation. However, he was found to be contributory negligent, and advised to abandon the claim. This left him with a hefty legal bill which caused his bankruptcy, with a liability of £79 17s 4d. (A secretary was on about 10s (50p) a week; and the price of a new piano started from 20 guineas (£21).)

After this you would have thought Greenwood would have stopped listening to people, but no. At the end of November, a notorious poacher from the area talked Greenwood into doing a bit of beating for him. They went onto the land of Mr. Leatham MP, and were caught. This landed him in the magistrate's court, but because it was Greenwood's first offence he was left off with paying the cost of 9s 6d (47½p).

Despite all the trouble at the end of 1868 Greenwood still managed to make a comeback at the beginning of the 1869 season for Yorkshire; this was against Nottinghamshire at Trent Bridge, Nottingham. He scored 24 runs (1 and 23) and took 2 wickets in the second innings. Greenwood played in another two matches for Yorkshire but he couldn't regain his true form.

Sadly their first child, Emma, died at the end of August 1869.

Greenwood later recalled the start of the 1870 season, for an exciting match he was involved in. It was against the MCC at

Lord's on May 30th 1870, with Yorkshire just managing to win by one wicket.

> They had 'brayed' us about a bit in the second innings, and we finally had only three wickets to go down and were about 70 or 80 runs behind. It looked all the world to a china orange against us. Myself, Tom Emmett, and the late John West had to go in. I soon lost my partner, and was joined by Tom. I began to hit very hard, and rattled up within a run or two of 50 while Tom was making nine. Then Tom ran me out and the game was a tie when John West came in. 'W.G.' and Alf Shaw were bowling, but Tom Emmett got the run, and we won by one wicket. I remember Tom saying, on coming out of the field, 'If we had los-end t' match ah sud nivver 'av shawn mi face in't pavilion for running thi' aht.'

Yorkshire Evening Post
December 4th 1897

During the match Greenwood only scored 2 runs in the first innings, but it was his 44 runs in the second innings that got him all the acclaim from the press.

> With the score at 80 for seven wickets, Luke Greenwood went to the wickets and by judicious play, good hitting, and timely running at a critical point of the game, he virtually won the match. The score rose to 93 when Wootton bowled Rawlinson for 13, including a good cut for three and a couple of fours. Eight wickets down and 51 wanted to win was the phase of the match when Emmett joined Greenwood. Emmett judiciously put the drag on his usual eager desire to hit, and amid a roar of cheers Greenwood lessened the M.C.C majority with a fine on-drive for 5, from Wootton. Then the score rose to 108 or 36 to win – when Shaw bowled from Wootton's end, and Mr. Grace bowled three overs at the other wicket; but no wicket falling, Wootton went on for the first time at the bottom wicket, but the score rose to 128, when Greenwood hit another 5 from the left-hander, a hearty and excited cheer greeting this fine hit which left the Yorkshire score at 133, or 11 to win. Then the new rule IX was enforced for the first time at Lord's, both Wootton and Shaw changing ends for a second time that innings; however, amid much excitement, a 3 by Greenwood, followed by a 3 by Emmett, made the score 143, and up stood the scorers proclaiming 'the tie'; then a smart bit of fielding ran out Greenwood for 44; and he retired amid loud and general applause. The batsmen's anxiety to win no doubt caused the run to be attempted, but it was an absurdly short one. West was now the last in and, amid breathless

silence, he played the remaining balls of Shaw's over. The first of Wootton's next over Emmett cut, got it past slip, and two were scored for it; thus finishing one of the best contested games ever seen at Lord's, Yorkshire winning by one wicket.

Huddersfield Weekly Examiner
June 4th 1870

While Luke was performing his heroics in London, his wife gave birth to their third child, Polly, on June 4th 1870. He was only picked to play one more match for Yorkshire that season.

Greenwood was still struggling to get to full fitness and he was only picked to play in two matches for Yorkshire in the 1871 season. His best performance was against Surrey at the Oval on August 21st. He scored 9 runs in the first innings, but he and Rowbotham helped Yorkshire win the match with a quick-fire 85 in the second innings, with Greenwood scoring 33 of them. He just managed to get back from London in time for the birth of his and Amelia's fourth child, Annie, who was born on August 31st 1871.

Greenwood only played two matches for Yorkshire again in the 1872 season, one of which he recalled because he managed to get one over W.G. Grace. Yorkshire where playing against Gloucestershire at Brammall Lane, Sheffield, on July 29th 1872. W.G. was knocking the Yorkshire bowlers all around the field, and the story goes as follows:

In the match W.G. thwacked me out of the field for six on the square-leg side. There used to be a practice in those days of giving a shilling to those who returned the lost balls. An old lady found this one, and toddled up with it to the wicket, as was the custom. She brought it to me, and I said 'Nah, yon's him that hit it; yo' mun go to him for t' brass.' She crossed the wicket to W.G. and gave him the ball, and he much amused, paid her the shilling forfeit.

Yorkshire Evening Post
December 4th 1897

Greenwood also narrated another tale about the match; in his reply to a telegram sent to him enquiring about the state of the game, he just said, 'We have not got a wicket yet, but are hoping to get one every day.' But Greenwood had the last word with help from his nephew;

Andrew caught W.G. from Luke's bowling for 150.

He only played two matches for Yorkshire in the 1873 season, and just before the second of those matches, which was against Nottinghamshire on August 28th 1873, the Greenwoods' fifth child, Grace, was born on August 27th. Luckily for Greenwood and Yorkshire, the match was at the Saint John's ground, Huddersfield, and he delighted his home crowd and showed Yorkshire just what they had been missing, taking 6 wickets for 65 runs (2-39 and 4-26).

Greenwood was not picked for the first match of the 1874 season, but he was brought back into the team for the rest of the season, and he was even made the captain and played in ten games that season, but there were no outstanding performances. Yorkshire also honoured Greenwood further by making the match against Gloucestershire at Brammall Lane, Sheffield, on July 27th 1874, his benefit match, and it managed to raise £300. (A dozen bottles of claret then cost 15s (75p); a dozen bottles of champagne cost 29s (£1.45); and tea was between 2s 4d (11.5p) and 3s (15p) per lb., depending on the blend.)

Yorkshire lost three of the ten games he captained that season – both the Gloucestershire games and one of the Lancashire games. But he was without Hill and Emmett for those games, and to add to his woes he only had ten men when Yorkshire played Gloucestershire at Clifton, Bristol, on August 13th 1874. Greenwood's captaincy was marked with a small write-up at the end of the season.

While Luke Greenwood, whenever he has had a chance, has shown us how, in his younger days, 'fields were won'. Captain Luke's modesty has generally led him to put himself in last, but even there he has often good service, as witness his 15 not out in the match with All England at St John's, and his 20 not out in the first match with Gloucestershire. Luke's captaincy has been very pleasant to everyone in the team.

Huddersfield Weekly Examiner
September 5th 1874

He played in just one match for Yorkshire in the 1875 season. This was towards the end of the season, and it was against

Chesterfield and District (Derbyshire) at Chesterfield on August 30th 1875, and he retired from county cricket at the end of the season.

GREENWOOD'S CAREER FIGURES:

Batting
Runs   1,006
Average 12.89

Bowling
Wickets 85
Runs   1,537
Average 18.08

Others
Catches 24

County Championships
1867, 1870

After his retirement, Greenwood became the landlord of the Carpenters Arms, Ossett, and he also became a well-respected umpire. He still kept in touch with Yorkshire and he was invited to play in the Yorkshire Gentlemen and Players match at the Savile ground, Dewsbury, on August 24th 1876.

In 1882 Greenwood was invited to be one of the umpires in the now infamous Test match between England and Australia at the Oval on August 28th. This match has gone into the record books as the first Ashes match. But Greenwood recalled it for an incident that involved his fellow umpire and what he called a bit of sharp practice by W.G. Grace.

> *There was an umpiring incident in the match, which I think has never been mentioned. It was a decision given by Bob Thomas. In the Australians' second innings, W.L. Murdoch and S.P. Jones were batting. Mr. Murdoch hit the ball a little on the leg side, and the Hon. A. Lyttleton, who was keeping wicket for England, ran for it and threw it in to Peate, who was at short slip. The run was made safely enough, and Peate made no attempt to take up the ball. Mr. Jones thereupon walked down out of his ground to pat the wicket where the ball had risen at the previous delivery, and W.G. Grace coolly picked up the ball, walked to the*

wicket, dislodged the bails, and cried, 'How's that?' Thomas, who was the umpire appealed to, gave him 'Out,' and out Mr. Jones had to go. Mr. Murdoch, on seeing what had occurred, remarked, 'That's very sharp practice, W.G.'; and to this day I think it was. Had I been appealed to I should not have given Jones out, for the ball was to all intents and purposes dead, and there had been no attempt to make a second run.

Yorkshire Evening Post
December 4th 1897

But according to the press it was the 'strictness, with which the game was played', and it was reported slightly differently.

Murdoch and Jones were together, when the captain made a hit to short leg. Mr. Lyttleton, the wicket keeper, fielded and threw in the ball, which was received by another member of the team and dropped at the wicket. The ball however, was not 'dead' – the wicket keeper having for the moment only acted as fielder; and Jones, forgetting this important fact, left his ground, and Mr. Grace, observing the movement, instantly picked up the ball and removed the bails. There was some momentary complaining on part of sympathisers with the colonists, but no kind of protest was made, or was possible.

Huddersfield Weekly Examiner
September 2nd 1882

But the antic backfired on Grace; it just spurred the Australians on in the field. With England just needing 85 runs to win, the Australians took every chance they got in the field, and England made what is by now a trademark collapse, and they lost the game by 7 runs.

Greenwood had to give up umpiring when his sight started to fail. Then his health started to deteriorate, and he lost the pub in 1896. Rumours soon started going round that Greenwood had wasted all the money on drink. But this was far from the truth. He was as professional behind the bar as he was on the cricket pitch, and only had a few drinks when he joined his old Lascelles Hall team-mates for their usual Christmas get-together at the Tandem, Waterloo. So at the age of 62, he was forced to try and make ends meet by digging up and laying new cricket pitches and tennis courts.

After the 'Old Ebor' articles – 'Talks With Old Cricketers' – in the *Yorkshire Evening Post* in December 1897, Greenwood was granted a pension by Yorkshire County Cricket Club, and they also used their influence to get him a lighter job as the groundsman at Morley Cricket Club. So the family moved to Fountain Street, Morley.

Their daughter, Polly, died at the end of April 1904, and on November 1st 1909 Luke Greenwood died at the age of 75. He was buried at Kirkheaton Graveyard on November 4th 1909. There was a headstone to mark his resting place, but it has been removed to make the churchyard look a bit better in wedding photos.

John Thewlis

John Thewlis's birth is a bit of a mystery because different records show different dates. I have used the date in the baptism records for this purpose, which states he was born at Hill Side, Heaton, on March 11th 1828. He was baptised at Kirkheaton Parish Church on April 16th 1828. He was the twelfth child of John and Frances Thewlis (née Kay), who were married at Kirkheaton Parish Church on October 2nd 1803. He had five brothers: Joseph, born in 1804; William, born in 1806; Charles, born in 1814; Abraham, born in 1817; and Benjamin, born in 1826. There were six sisters: Mary, born in 1809; Elizabeth, born in 1811; Sarah, born in 1819; Jane, born in 1821; Harriet, born in 1824; and Frances, born in 1825.

With all those children in a small two-roomed weaver's cottage, I would imagine space was a bit hard to come by and money would have been even scarcer. John refused to go to school because the other children bullied him about his white hair; however, he still managed to teach himself how to read and write. At a young age he started to work with the family as a weaver, like most children did in those days.

Thewlis was friends with Luke Greenwood, and they played cricket together in local, representative and Yorkshire sides. On one occasion it was said that Lascelles Hall dropped him, so he went to a nearby field to practise his batting. While he was practising, the team that was due to play Lascelles Hall stopped him and asked him the whereabouts of the Lascelles Hall ground, so Thewlis promptly gave them directions to the ground. On noticing how well he played, the captain of the team enquired politely on departing, 'if he would be on the field against them that day?' Thewlis promptly replied, 'No, I aren't good enough to play with that lot!' And with that answer, the team just turned round and went home.

Once John's brothers and sisters started getting married and moving out, the cottage was getting a bit more spacious. But with the death of his mother, Frances, on March 24th 1847, and with his father's eyesight starting to fail him, it was decided to let the cottage go, and they accepted an invitation to move in with his sister, Jane, and her new husband, Charles Lockwood, and their son, Ephraim.

Thewlis accepted an offer to become a professional cricketer with Glossop. While he was there, he was invited to play in a match at Oldham and when the opposition saw him and J. Bowers having a knockabout before the game, they decided not to play, and they went back home without playing. Also during his spell with Glossop, Thewlis met Mary Batty, and they were married at Littlemoor Chapel, on November 16th 1856.

It is said he was first picked to play for a Yorkshire representative side in 1861, but without being able to look at the early records I cannot be sure when. However, I do know he played for a Yorkshire side alongside his brother-in-law, J. Berry, against Surrey at Sheffield in July 1862.

With the formation of the new Yorkshire County Cricket Club, Thewlis was picked for their first match, which was against Surrey at the Oval, on June 4th 1963. Thewlis opened for Yorkshire and he managed to score 17 runs; he also took 2 catches. In Yorkshire's first home match, which was against Nottinghamshire at Great Horton Lane, Bradford, on June 22nd 1863, after his poor performance at Surrey, Thewlis's name was said to be the last one entered on the team sheet. This time he made most of the opportunity, and he was the top scorer with 46 runs in the first innings, and he got 16 runs in the second innings.

Thewlis was in and out of the Yorkshire side for most of his career, but this didn't stop him having faith in his own ability to play the game. He later recalled he was made to regret this faith when he challenged eleven landlords at Chickenley to a match.

I remember once playing an eleven single-handed myself, and I don't remember any other Yorkshireman having done a similar feat. I offered to play eleven landlords residing within a mile of Chickenley. Included in the eleven were several men of local cricketing experience. The match came off on the present Dewsbury and Savile ground. We had a long disputation as to the method of scoring, but finally I carried my point that all runs were to be made in front of the wicket. I only got one run in the first innings, but in the second innings they could not get me out and the match was drawn. I

*had an awful lot of running about in the match, and got so knocked up that
I said I would never attempt such another task in my life.*

Yorkshire Evening Post
December 18th 1897

Thewlis regularly toured the country with different All England
sides, but he always enjoyed playing in front of the local
supporters. He showed his appreciation for their support on June
30th 1866 when he formed an all-Thewlis XI from Lascelles Hall
to play against Chickenley, and the crowd showed their
appreciation for his innings when he returned to the pavilion.

*John Thewlis contributed 98 in a hard-hitting innings. On his return to
the pavilion he was presented with a small acknowledgement for his fine
display of cricket, in the shape of money, gathered among the spectators.*

Huddersfield Weekly Examiner
July 7th 1866

Thewlis played in four matches for Yorkshire when they won the
County Championship for the first time in 1867.

In the 1868 season Thewlis played in five matches for Yorkshire,
and he was also picked to play for the Players against the Gentlemen
at the Oval July 7th. However, the year was noted more for his
performance in Yorkshire's last county game, which was against
Surrey at the Oval on August 24th. Due to an accident at
Nottingham involving a couple of the Yorkshire players, Yorkshire
were short of a player, and Thewlis was asked if he knew of a good
man, so he recommended his nephew, E. Lockwood. But he wasn't
the only one to recommend someone, as he later recalled.

*I said I had a young one I could recommend, Eph. Lockwood, then at
Cheetham Hill. Roger Iddison wanted to give a trial to Milner Gibson,
and there was opposition between Iddison and I as to getting our men in.
Mr. Pedley at last asked, 'Is there anyone that knows this lad of yours,
John?' and I replied that Tom Emmett did. Tom said, 'Aye, Eph.
Lockwood is a good one,' and thus it was that Ephraim was sent for.*

Yorkshire Evening Post
December 18th 1897

Surrey were all out for 195, and Thewlis came out to open the Yorkshire innings with his nephew at about 4.15 p.m. Thewlis was dropped on 23 and Yorkshire finished the day on 109 for 0. Thewlis and Lockwood came out on August 25th, and they had put on 176 when Lockwood was caught and bowled by Bristow. Thewlis went on and he got the first century by a Yorkshire player in a county match; it was also the only century of his county career. He was finally caught by Pooley off the bowling of Griffith for 109 (1-8, 4-4, 6-3, 15-2 and the rest in singles). The achievement was reported rather sedately:

A really sound cricketer's innings and he was much applauded for his splendid inning.

Huddersfield Weekly Examiner
August 29th 1868

That performance helped Thewlis to be top of the batting averages for Yorkshire at the end of the season.

Despite his finish to the 1868 season, Yorkshire overlooked him for the 1869 season.

Thewlis was picked for all the Yorkshire games in the 1870 season, but he only managed to get 269 runs, with a top score of 61 runs.

He was overlooked by Yorkshire in the 1871 season, and he was only picked for one game in the 1872 season.

Thewlis must have thought his career with Yorkshire was over, but towards the end of the 1873 season he was picked to play against Surrey at the Oval on August 11th, and he scored 50 runs in his first and only innings.

He was picked for four matches in the 1874 season. He scored 191 runs in the season, and his highest score was 62 runs, which was made against Sussex at Brighton.

Yorkshire had a benefit match for him against Gloucestershire, at Brammall Lane, Sheffield, on July 26th 1875, which raised £350. (A bottle of whisky under 33° proof cost 2s 3d (11p); old whisky was 3s 3d (16p); 2-year-old port was 1s 3d (6p), and 5-year-old port was 1s 9d (9p).) A report about Thewlis's career was in the local paper on the day the match commenced.

To-day, the match, Yorkshire v. Gloucester, is to be played at Brammall Lane Ground, Sheffield, for the benefit of John Thewlis. During his whole career (says the Sporting Life*) there has not been a quieter or more unobtrusive player than Thewlis. As a batsman he has manfully upheld the honour of his county for many years. His long-stopping was always very fine, and even now this position in the field is generally allotted to him. It can scarcely be expected that now, when he is close bordering on fifty years of age, he can display the same agility as in his early career, but his performance even now in that position is difficult to excel. As a batsman he was much in request for some time as an engaged man against the different All-England teams, which contest brought him into notoriety some thirteen years ago. His first great performance was for the North v. South in 1864, when he was top scorer for the side with 77 and 21. For several years he maintained his well-earned reputation as a safe batsman. In 1868 he achieved his greatest success, when he and his kinsman, Ephraim Lockwood, who made his debut at the Oval in that year, went in first, and scored 176 before they were separated, whilst Thewlis in all made 108. For three years he was mostly on the shelf, but in 1873 and 1874 he came back again, and last year played as brilliant as in his palmiest days, holding the third position in his county, with an excellent average of 23.7. It is unnecessary to recapitulate his doings this year, which have been more than meritorious.*

Huddersfield Daily Examiner
July 26th 1875

The runs started to elude him and he only managed to score 84 runs in the 1875 season, and this turned out to be his last year with Yorkshire.

THEWLIS'S CAREER FIGURES:

Batting
Runs   1,313
Average   15.44
Centuries   1

Others
Catches   21
Stumpings   1

County Championships
1867, 1870

After he finished playing Thewlis went back to life as a fancy weaver, but with the ups and downs of the weaving trade he was forced to move around to find work and make a living. He ended up living in obscurity in a four-roomed house in Failsworth, which is in the Oldham area of Lancashire. He was just managing to keep the wolf from the door by carrying heavy laundry baskets to Manchester, and taking in lodgers. He was tracked down by 'Old Ebor', who was doing his series of articles for the *Yorkshire Evening Post* entitled 'Talks With Old Cricketers'. Old Ebor was so appalled by the way Thewlis was forced to make a living he subtitled the article 'The Vicissitudes of Old Age', and made a scathing attack on the Yorkshire County Cricket Club.

The writer of these articles wishes to preface the interview with John Thewlis with a little plain speaking. The position in which a few of Yorkshire's old cricketers have been found in the search for these interviews is not an agreeable testimony to the influence of cricket itself upon the fortunes of those who adopted it as a profession. Still less is it creditable to Yorkshire County Cricket Club. The moral responsibilities of cricket managers, so far as a player is concerned, should surely not end with the termination of his career. He ought not to be cast aside like an old shoe.

This is what Yorkshire has done with some of the fathers of the county's cricket. Men received their benefit, such as it was, dropped out of the team, and were forgotten. Possibly but for these interviews they would have remained in obscurity until their death. It is no exaggeration to say that one or two might have died in want without the public being aware of their necessities. It is necessary, therefore, to protest strongly and publicly against the way in which a few old Yorkshire cricketers have been allowed to sink into oblivion, and even into poverty. One would have thought that the kindly remembrance of past services would at least have enabled the Yorkshire County Club to know whether old players were under the sod or above it. Inquiries in a quarter where knowledge might have been expected concerning the whereabouts of John Thewlis elicited the reply, 'Think dead; if not, Manchester!'

John Thewlis is not dead. He is living at No. 782, Oldham Road, Failsworth, near Manchester.

Yorkshire Evening Post
December 18th 1897

A bit further on in the article he wrote:

John Thewlis, in his 70th year, is 'on the rocks'. His wife told the writer that they struggle to live, and that if some light employment could be found for her husband, they would be very grateful. This is a matter to which the responsible managers of Yorkshire cricket should have their attentions directed. Meanwhile I have given the kind reader John Thewlis's address; and next Saturday is Christmas Day.

Thewlis will be 70 years of age on January 30 next. He is looking well, and can do his 20-mile walk a day now. 'In fact,' he said, 'I think I could play cricket now but for my sight. I have had to cease going to matches because I could not see what was taking place at the wicket. I am perfectly sound and healthy but for this. I have lost my teeth, but it's perhaps as well I have, for there hasn't been much for them to do lately.'

Yorkshire Evening Post
December 18th 1897

This gave the Yorkshire Committee the jolt they needed, and a meeting was called and they granted him a pension of 10s (50p) per week. (India pale ale was 1s 9d (9p) per dozen half-pint bottles; whisky was 3s 6d (17.5p) and Brooke Bond tea cost between 10d (4p) and 2s (10p) per lb., depending on the blend.)

This pension was sadly short-lived, though. The following winter, while he was visiting friends and relatives for Christmas, John Thewlis died at the Tandem Inn, Waterloo, Huddersfield, at the age of 71, on December 29th 1899. He was buried in the public section of the Kirkheaton Churchyard new ground on January 1st 1900. It was said that the players of the Lascelles Hall cricket club were so appalled about the nature of the grave that they had a whip-round and they soon collected enough money to pay for a headstone to mark his grave. But the public section of the churchyard is near to a stream, so therefore the ground is a bit boggy. The headstone was soon deemed unsafe and it had to be removed.

Ephraim Lockwood

Ephraim Lockwood was born on April 4th 1845, and baptised at Kirkheaton Parish Church on September 19th 1845. He was the first child of Charles and Jane Lockwood (née Thewlis). His father was a weaver, and they were married at Kirkheaton Church on March 7th 1844. They had four more children: three boys, David, born in 1848, George, born in 1853, and Henry, born in 1856; and one girl, Mary, born in 1850 (but she died young). They lived in a small weaver's cottage in Lascelles Hall, near the Hills and the Greenwoods. His grandfather and uncle John Thewlis moved in with them after the death of his grandmother in 1847, but after the death of his mother, Jane, at the age of 38 in May 1859, they moved in with another uncle.

With Ephraim growing up near his uncles and the Greenwoods it was no surprise he started playing cricket. He spent a lot of his spare time practising, and in the article 'Talks With Old Cricketers' he described how they used to practise in the early days:

> *We used to do a lot of practice on the road with seat-board legs and yarn balls. Don't know what seat-board legs are! Ah, you didn't know the old hand-looms weavers. Seat-board legs were sticks that used to support the hand-loom weavers' seats. Practice! When I was a lad we were always at it. We had scarcely time to swallow our meals; indeed, I don't mind confessing that I have occasionally dined on a turnip rather than break away from good practice.*

Yorkshire Evening Post
November 27th 1897

He started playing for the Lascelles Hall club as a lad, but Lockwood was first engaged as a professional by Kirkburton in about 1865. He then moved to Meltham in 1866, and then he went to Lockwood in 1867, then to Cheetham Hill, Manchester

1868, and it was while he was there he got the call from Yorkshire.

After an omnibus crashed with some Yorkshire players on board, Yorkshire were struggling to find a team for the Surrey match at the Oval on August 24th 1868, and it was suggested by his uncle, John Thewlis, that they give him a chance. Lockwood was wired at Cheetham Hill, but he was in Huddersfield, getting ready to play in a match for Lascelles Hall, at Yeadon. Luckily the message was forwarded to Huddersfield, and he managed to get to London in time for the match.

Yorkshire decided to open the innings with Lockwood and his uncle, John, Lockwood made 91 runs in an opening partnership of 176 runs. At first his attire seemed to have more of an impact on the crowd than he did.

Lockwood went on to the field in a pair of trousers that had run in the washing, and a shirt with red, black, and green squares like a church window. He looked a raw lad, but he was not so raw as he looked.

Huddersfield Weekly Examiner
December 24th 1921

That performance was good enough for Yorkshire to give him a more permanent place in the 1869 season.

Lockwood was now taking a liking to the Oval ground, and he got his first century (103) for Yorkshire against Surrey at the Oval on August 5th 1869, and he made 34 not out in the second innings. At the end of the season, Lockwood married Harriet Hirst at Kirkheaton Parish Church on September 28th 1869, and they moved to Common End, Lascelles Hall.

At the beginning of the 1870 season Lockwood played a vital part in a match for Yorkshire when they beat Nottinghamshire at Trent Bridge on June 23rd 1870, by 2 runs. G. Freeman had broken down earlier on in the game and R. Iddison didn't want to risk T. Emmett bowling a wide, so he told Lockwood to bowl from consecutive ends. It proved to be inspirational captaincy, and Lockwood took the last wicket and Yorkshire won the game by 2 runs.

In the 1871 season, Lockwood played another key role for Yorkshire; but this time it was with the bat and in the dark, against Surrey at Brammall Lane, Sheffield, on June 19th, scoring 89 runs in the second innings.

> *Lockwood, although the light was bad during almost the whole time he was in, and once it was so gloomy as to cause a suspension of play, played a magnificent innings of 89, in which were five 3's, and eighteen 2's. He only gave one chance, when he had scored 65, and his playing of Southerton's peculiar slows was a fine display of batting skill. When he was finally disposed of the ground was enveloped in dense gloom.*

Huddersfield Weekly Examiner
June 24th 1871

Lockwood was picked for the Players against the Gentlemen in the second of the matches at Lord's on July 3rd 1871, and he was the top scorer with 76 runs.

Lockwood was having a good 1872 season, and towards the end of the season he had another good innings against Surrey at the Oval on August 8th. He scored 121 runs and got all the accolades in the press:

> *The great feature of the match was the brilliant innings of Lockwood, whose steady defence and effective hitting were greatly admired. The* Daily News, *referring to Lockwood, says: 'His brilliant career was brought to a conclusion by a catch at short leg at five minutes before one. His correct and splendid innings of 121 contained such items as a six, four fours, twelve threes, fifteen twos etc, and he was loudly and deservedly cheered by all present for his admirable display of perfection in the batting art.'*

Huddersfield Weekly Examiner
August 10th 1872

Lockwood finished top of the batting averages for Yorkshire at the end of the 1872 season.

He was by now becoming a good sturdy batter and when he scored 66 not out in the first innings for the Players against the Gentlemen, at the Oval on July 2nd 1874, he became the first man to carry his bat through an innings in such games. He followed it up with 48 runs in the second. He even outshone the legendary W.G. Grace in the four Gentlemen against Players matches in 1874-1875; Lockwood was the top scorer in the matches scoring 326 runs at an average of 40.75 (W.G. was second with 299 runs at an average of 37.37).

Towards the end of the 1875 season, Lockwood showed he could still turn his arm over and he took 8 wickets for 59 runs (2-33 and 6-26) against Middlesex at Brammall Lane, Sheffield, on August 9th. He finished the season third in both the batting and bowling averages for Yorkshire.

Yorkshire appointed him as the captain in 1876, but the county only finished third and Lockwood only managed to score 254 runs in the season.

The 1877 season was even worse for Yorkshire, and they only finished seventh. However, Lockwood had a better season with the bat, and he finished the season with 432 runs, and even managed to pick up 11 wickets. During the season he got the chance to play alongside his brother, Harry, when he made his county debut, against Middlesex at Lord's on June 4th 1877; but G. Pinder remembered the match for another reason.

> *Like many wicket keepers, Pinder could bowl at a pinch. 'In one match Yorkshire v. Middlesex,' he said, 'in the Old Prince's ground London, Allan Hill and five other bowlers could do no good and we looked like having a bad licking. Eph Lockwood was captain, and I said to him, "let me try those little uns of mine." He let me have my way and took the wicket himself. The result was that in the last over before lunch I got the wickets of the brothers Webbe, and the first over after lunch D. Eastwood missed a catch off me. We won the match however, and Lord Londesborough was so delighted that he sent for Lockwood and I to visit him at his house in Berkeley Square, when he congratulated us on Yorkshire's victory, and presented me with £3 and Lockwood with £2.'*

Yorkshire Evening Post
January 1st 1898

Despite that match, Lockwood was replaced by T. Emmett as the Yorkshire captain for the 1878 season, and at first it seem to lift Lockwood's form. He scored another century for Yorkshire; this time it was against Gloucestershire at Brammall Lane, Sheffield, on July 29th. But he finished the season with just two more runs than the season before, and he only took 5 wickets.

His wife, Harriet, sadly died on March 23rd, just as he was getting ready for the 1879 season. She was just 29. Understandably, Lockwood had a poor season, only managing to score 278 runs, with his highest score being 39 runs.

At the end of the season Lockwood accepted an invitation by Daft to tour Canada and America. They departed on August 28th 1879. Lockwood caused a bit of a stir at the beginning of the tour. On a visit to Niagara Falls when he was asked what he thought about the scenery he replied, 'If that's Niagara Falls I'd rather have Lascelles Hall.' Lockwood didn't have an over-successful tour and only started to hit form at the end of the trip. They sailed back to England on October 27th 1879, and this turned out to be the only time Lockwood toured abroad.

Lockwood's form with the bat came back in the 1880 season, and at the end of the season he had scored 610 runs.

Lockwood's consistency was back, and at the beginning of the 1881 season he scored 109 runs in Yorkshire's first innings against Surrey in front of his home crowd at Fartown, Huddersfield, on June 2nd 1881.

Lockwood was greatly cheered when he completed his hundred. He had reached 109, when in attempting to drive Porter, he put the ball up to Shutter at cover point. His innings was almost perfect in his defence and hitting, his cutting being effective and pretty in the extreme.

Huddersfield Weekly Examiner
June 4th 1881

He finished the 1881 season with 785 runs, which was his highest total of runs for Yorkshire in a season, and Lockwood, or 'Old Mary Ann' as he was now known, found time to play a practical joke on E. Peate, as Peate later recalled.

We were playing in Gents v. Players at the Oval, when I carelessly left my watch on the dressing room table at the hotel, with the bedroom door open. Eph. Lockwood passing at the time, hopped in and carefully put the watch in his pocket – for safety. When I could not find it I was under the impression that it had been 'sneaked' on the ground. Lord Harris, W.G. Grace, and the others condoled with me on my loss, and Eph. Lockwood and my other pals went with me to Scotland Yard to report it. We roused all Scotland Yard up nearly, and I was busy for about a fortnight making inquiries about my missing watch. At last, when I thought I had seen the last of it, Ephraim quietly handed it over to me as if nothing had happened. He and the others had had a fortnight's quiet chuckling at my expense.

Yorkshire Evening Post
April 2nd 1898

Lockwood was booked to go on the winter tour of Australia in 1881, but due to an attack of acute rheumatism he had to cancel. He didn't waste his time. In the winter, he married Fanny Lucy Brown, who was the widowed niece of Fuller Pilcer (a former Kent cricketer), at Saint Barnabas' Church, Sheffield, on December 12th 1881, and they opened a sports outfitters in Moldgreen, Huddersfield.

Lockwood started the 1882 season well, and the local paper started to get behind him and asking for him to be picked for the England teams.

In his four innings against the Australians, Lockwood has made 122 runs, and has been not out twice. He certainly ought to be included in the All England Players Team that will meet the colonials at the oval.

Huddersfield Weekly Examiner
June 14th 1882

Yorkshire also repaid him by holding a benefit match for him, which was against Lancashire at Brammall Lane, Sheffield, on July 24th 1882, and a special train was put on from Huddersfield for the match. The fare was 2s 6d (12.5p) third class return; the benefit raised £591 0s 7d. (Coffee was 1s 4d (6.5p) per lb. and a fast steamer to America was £4 10s (£4. 50).)

The powers that be listened to the public, and they invited Lockwood to play for the Players of England against the Australian XI at the Oval on August 10th 1882; he was also made the captain. He repaid their faith in him by leading the Players to an innings and 34 runs victory. Lockwood remembered the match for an incident that made his wife chuckle.

She was sitting in the reserved seats at the pavilion, near where three gaily-attired society young ladies were seated. The young ladies criticised us poor players with unblushing frankness. 'Do you know who that is?' said one to the other. 'Yes; why, that's Punch,' was the reply. 'Punch' was Tom Emmett. 'Who's that one there?' 'That's Big Feet.' Big Feet was poor me. 'Who's the other?' 'That's the dashing young Yorkshireman.' The player thus favoured was Billy Bates. My wife, having heard all the conversation, enjoyed the situation hugely when Punch, Big Feet, and the Dashing One walked from the field to the pavilion to talk to her. The young ladies looked fit to sink into their shoes on knowing that their candid comments must have been heard.

Yorkshire Evening Post
November 27th 1897

Due to the Australians thinking Lockwood had snubbed them the previous winter, it was decided not to pick Lockwood for the England Test side that was due to play the Australian side he had just defeated at the Oval. The Test was at the Oval and started on August 28th 1882, and England duly lost the game, and the death of English cricket was announced in the *Sporting Times*.

While the debate was going on in the South about what was wrong with English cricket, Lockwood showed it wasn't quite that dead in the North, scoring another century for Yorkshire. He scored 104 not out against the I Zingari XI at Scarborough on September 4th 1882, and the cap was passed round and raised £11. He was then the top scorer with 53 runs when the North of England beat the Australians by 10 wickets at Old Trafford on September 14th 1882.

Lockwood's batting was just getting better and better, and against Kent at the Bat and Ball ground, Gravesend, on August 16th 1883, Lockwood scored 208 runs, which was his highest score for Yorkshire.

Lockwood remained at the wicket until within a few minutes of the time for drawing stumps, when he was caught by the wicketkeeper standing back. He was batting while 297 runs were scored and by splendid cricket made 208. His hitting all round was admirable, and his defence excellent. His innings included twenty-three 4s, nine 3s and twenty-two 2s. It is worthy of note that this is the largest score Lockwood has ever made in his long career as a cricketer.

Huddersfield Weekly Examiner
August 20th 1883

It was also the first time a double century had been scored by a Yorkshire batter in a county match.

Lockwood finished the season with 559 runs, and ironically he finished the top of the bowling averages for Yorkshire, by taking just 1 wicket for 9 runs against Gloucestershire at Gloucester on July 12th 1883. It was the only time he bowled in the season, giving him an average of 9.

In 1884 Lockwood's rheumatism was getting worse and he only managed to play in three matches in the season, only scoring 34 runs, with a highest score of 10 runs; and at the end of the season 1884 he decided to retire from first class cricket.

LOCKWOOD'S CAREER FIGURES:

Batting
Runs   7,868
Average   23.27
Centuries   6
Double Centuries 1

Bowling
Wickets   141
Runs   2,273
Average   16.12

Others
Catches   164
Stumpings   2

County Championships
1870

The Lockwoods moved their sports shop to bigger premises at 18 West Parade, Huddersfield, near the town centre and the station. He started making cricket bats with his stepson, and he became the sole agent for Gray and Son tennis racquets in Huddersfield. He didn't give up playing cricket, though, and he signed for the Dalton Cricket Club in the 1885 season.

They had a son, Ephraim, in July 1887, but unfortunately he only lived fifteen weeks and died on October 25th 1887.

When his friend and old team-mate, Billy Bates, tried to

commit suicide at the beginning of 1889, Lockwood went straight round to see him and offer his support to him and his family. His father, Charles, died later in the year at the age of 69, on November 6th 1889.

Lockwood was still active on the cricket field, and he was the captain of Lascelles Hall in 1891 when they won the Heavy Woollen Cup at the first attempt, after it was decided to enter the cup following a row about the use of professionals in the Lumb Cup.

Lockwood's health started to deteriorate, and to make things worse his eyesight started to fail him. Lockwood was confined to bed with bronchitis in the November of 1921, and it was decided it would be better if he moved in with his brother, Harry, back at Tandem, Lepton. Sadly, Ephraim Lockwood died shortly after on December 19th 1921, at the good age of 76. He was buried at Edgerton Cemetery (consecrated), Huddersfield, on December 22nd 1921, but there is nothing to mark the life of one of the greatest Yorkshire cricketers the area as produced.

It seems apt to finish with the following tribute written by W.G. Grace, which was part of Lockwood's obituary, entitled 'Death of One of Yorkshire's Greatest Batsmen'.

He was one of the best all-round players of his time, batting with success and fielding with great certainty. He was not a brilliant batsman, nor particularly free in his style, but what he lacked in that respect he made up in patience and carefulness. His bat was always in the way of the ball, and he had few superiors in watching and timing all kinds of bowling on a rough and kicking wicket. He could hit anywhere, his cut being particularly fine; and he had one peculiar stroke, which I used to consider a mis-hit for a long time. Off slow bowling he made what seemed a half-hearted hit just over the bowler's or mid-off's head, but which did not go far enough for long field to reach. Time after time a catch seemed likely to come off, but the fieldsman was always a yard or two short, which was very tantalising, and I was compelled to conclude that the hit, though not pretty to look at was intentional, especially as he scored by it every time.

On a wet or dead wicket he was seen at his best; then he could watch the ball for any length of time, keeping up his wicket with a very straight bat, and putting on the runs at a fair pace when others failed to score.

Huddersfield Weekly Examiner
December 24th 1921

Andrew Greenwood

Andrew Greenwood was born on August 20th 1847, he was the only child of Job Thornton Greenwood and Ann Greenwood (née Whittle), who were married at Kirkheaton on August 22nd 1845. His father was a hand-loom weaver, and one of the earliest professional cricketers to come out of the Lascelles Hall cricket club, he was classed as a good player, but he never had the opportunity to play for Yorkshire. Andrew grew up in Lascelles Hall and became a hand-loom weaver.

Greenwood started playing cricket at an early age alongside his uncles and cousins at Lascelles Hall, and at the age of seventeen he was good enough to play alongside his father and Uncle Luke for Harrogate against an All England XI.

Greenwood's first appearance in a county match for Yorkshire was in the opening match of the 1869 season. It was against Nottingham at Trent Bridge on May 31st 1869, alongside his uncle, Luke, and E. Lockwood, but he failed to have an impact on the game. He got a duck in the first innings and only scored 8 runs in the second; he wasn't given another chance to play in a county match that season.

Greenwood was only involved in one county match in the 1870 season. This was against Surrey at Sheffield, on August 8th, and again he failed to show his true ability. At the end of the season, Greenwood was picked to play for the Yorkshire Colts against the United North on September 9th. This time he managed to show some of his potential; he scored 21 runs in the first innings and he was top scorer in the second innings with 55 not out.

Greenwood was given a better chance to prove himself in the Yorkshire first team in the 1871 season. He was picked for six county matches, and he finished the season with 203 runs at an average of 18.5. His best performance came against Lancashire at Old Trafford, on June 29th 1871, scoring 21 not out in the first innings and 50 runs in the second.

The 1872 season was a bit of a stop and start one for Greenwood. He only got 1 run and 14 runs in the opening match against Middlesex at the Prince's ground on May 23rd. He picked up 2 ducks against Gloucestershire at Brammall Lane, Sheffield on July 29th, with W.G. Grace taking his wicket both times; then against Surrey he only scored 6 runs. Despite these poor performances he still managed to get his name on the sheet for the North against South, and he repaid their faith in him by having two of his best matches that season. He scored 52 runs in his only innings in the first match at Canterbury on August 6th 1872. He then got all the acclaim in the return match at the Woodhouse Hill ground, Hunslet, on August 8th. After a patient start to the first innings he finished the top scorer with 69 runs.

A. Greenwood took to the wicket, and for the first two or three overs found quite sufficient occupation in the defence of his wicket. Rowbotham also played with extreme caution. Presently however, the bowling became more loose, and both batsmen set to work and there was an exhibition of fine and free batting, which kept the spectators almost incessantly applauding. Greenwood sent the ball to all parts of the field, and soon, not content with this, made a superb leg hit of Silcock clear out of the ground, some forty or fifty yards into an adjoining field, from which he was credited with 6. After putting on a brace of 2's and three singles, he repeated the performance, to the great delight of the spectators, one of whom declared that the ball 'had gone to Huddersfield'.

Huddersfield Daily Examiner
August 9th 1872

Greenwood went on to further cement his place in the Yorkshire side in the 1873 season. He was also invited to play for the Players against the Gentlemen for the first time in the second game, which was at the Oval on July 3rd, where he scored 28 runs and 8 runs. This was a good experience for him, and when he returned to the Yorkshire team he scored 68 runs against Sussex at Brammall Lane, Sheffield, on July 14th.

Greenwood was now growing in confidence and Brammall Lane was fast becoming his favourite ground. He got his highest score of the season at the ground, which was 89 runs in the second innings against his old nemesis, W.G. Grace, and his Gloucestershire side on

July 28th 1873. Then against Nottinghamshire 18 August 1873 he managed to do one of W.G.'s tricks and scored a run before he took the field on the 19th.

> *Greenwood's score was altered this morning, it being found out that three were run on Monday when the umpire called out two only.*

Huddersfield Weekly Examiner
August 23rd 1873

He finished the season second in the batting averages for Yorkshire with an average of 20.4, scoring 500 runs from 13 matches.

As the season was coming to a close, Greenwood married Alice Ann Townsend at Halifax Parish Church, on September 25th 1873. But the honeymoon had to be a short one, because he had accepted an invitation by W.G. Grace to tour Australia in the winter of 1873-74. It was not an over-successful tour for Greenwood, who finished with an average of only 15.

On his return from the Antipodes on about May 18th 1874, Greenwood had a good start to the new season for Yorkshire, and when they played Surrey at Brammall Lane on June 15th, he was in top form, scoring 77 runs and 38 runs. Greenwood was invited to play for England against Kent and Gloucestershire at the Canterbury Festival on August 3rd 1874, and W.G. Grace was now bringing the best out of him. He managed to score 53 and 31 runs, but W.G. still got his wicket both times. One of Greenwood's best performances for Yorkshire was in the second innings against Gloucestershire at Clifton, Bristol, on August 13th. With Yorkshire only being able to field ten men, and W.G. Grace in fine form, Greenwood managed to hold out, and he scored 34 runs in the first innings and was 78 not out in the second innings.

> *Yorkshire's first three wickets (Smith's, Shotton's, and Lockwood's) fell for 17 runs. Andrew Greenwood came to the rescue, and after giving a chance to Mr. Knapp at long-off, he went on scoring. Emmett and Ulyett succumbed early, but Mr. Byram, with Thewlis and Clayton, aided Andrew Greenwood in sturdily batting against the odds, till Luke*

Huddersfield Daily Examiner
August 17th 1874

At the end of the 1874 season, he was Yorkshire's second top run scorer to Lockwood, with 445 runs from 12 matches at an average of 22.5.

Greenwood started the 1875 season well. Against Middlesex at the Prince's ground on May 20th, he scored 3 runs and 50 runs. Greenwood stopped down there for the North against South match at the Prince's ground on May 27th and got 39 runs and 93 runs.

When he returned from London, the Greenwoods celebrated the birth of their first child, Blanche Evelyn, on June 5th 1875.

Greenwood had to cut the celebration short to play for Yorkshire against Surrey at Brammall Lane, Sheffield, on June 14th. He got his highest score of the season, which was 61 runs, and he followed it up with 40 not out. Greenwood then went back to London to play for the Players against the Gentlemen at the Oval on July 1st 1875, and scored 30 runs and 14 runs. In the second game at Lord's on July 5th, he did a bit better, scoring 52 runs and 24 runs, but it was W.G. who took his wicket three times.

He again finished the second highest run scorer for Yorkshire; he was pipped by Lockwood again.

Greenwood only played 8 matches for Yorkshire in the 1876 season, only scoring 212 runs. But he didn't disappoint his home crowd when he played in the North against South match at the Saint John's ground, Huddersfield, on July 13th. He was batting so well that the only way they could get him out was with a bit of sharp work in the field, but that wasn't until he had scored 111 runs. The papers seem more interested in an incident at the beginning of the North's innings, which involved W.G. Grace trying to unsettle the opening batters, than Greenwood's century:

On resumption after the South were all out for 102; There was now another interval, which was made a little longer than was necessary by an objection raised by Mr. W.G. to the umpires wearing white jackets during the innings of the North, on the ground that they had not worn them when the South were batting, and although there were cries of 'play' by the spectators, he was obdurate until Lockwood ordered them not to be used.

Huddersfield Daily Examiner
July 14th 1876

Shortly after that game, their second child, Florence Ethel, was born 1 August 1876. Despite his fairly poor season, Greenwood was still picked by Lillywhite for the 1876-77 winter tour of the Antipodes.

It was a hard tour, and towards the end Greenwood was picked to play against the Combined Melbourne and Sydney XI at the Melbourne Cricket Ground on March 15th 1877. It was not a great game for Greenwood, he only scored 1 run in the first innings and 5 runs in the second, and only taking one catch; but that match is now regarded as the first Test match to take place between two cricketing countries.

Greenwood started the 1877 season slowly, but he finished it strongly. When Yorkshire played Gloucestershire at Sheffield on July 30th, he didn't let the Brammall Lane faithful down, and he just failed to carry his bat through the first innings. He opened the innings for Yorkshire and his was the last wicket to fall, and he got his highest county score of 91 runs. It was also the top score in the match and this milestone was marked with just a few words in the paper.

His magnificent score of 91 was obtained by thoroughly sound and good cricket.

Huddersfield Daily Examiner
August 1st 1877

He only managed to get 5 runs in the second innings. He scored 49 runs in his only innings against Middlesex at Brammall Lane on August 13th 1877, and he scored 75 runs in his only innings against Derbyshire at Derby on August 20th. At the end of the season, Greenwood finished top of the Yorkshire batting averages, with 386 runs at an average of 25.11.

The Greenwoods took over the running of the Crown Hotel, Holmfirth, and his mother and father moved in with them to help out when he was away playing cricket. Their third child, Charles Lewis, was born on April 22nd 1878, but Greenwood was now suffering more and more from rheumatic gout, which was the curse of the early cricketers. He only managed to play in 8 matches in the 1878 season, scoring just 167 runs, and he didn't manage to play at all for Yorkshire in the 1879 season.

Sadly, their son, Charles Lewis, died on September 26th 1879; but shortly after the funeral, their fourth child, Arthur Edward, was born on November 12th 1879.

Greenwood only played one match for Yorkshire in the 1880 season, which was in a rain-affected game against Australia at the Fartown Ground, Huddersfield, on July 22nd 1880, and in his last innings for Yorkshire he was out for a duck. With the rheumatism getting worse, Greenwood now decided to retire from first class cricket at the end of the 1880 season.

GREENWOOD'S CAREER FIGURES:

Batting
County Runs   2,780
Average   17.82
Test Runs   77
Average   19.25

Others
County Catches 33
Test Catches   2

County Championship
1870

The Greenwoods moved to the Peacock Inn in Holbeck, and then to the White Hart Hotel in Liversedge. They finally moved back to Huddersfield in 1887, when they took over the running of the

Black Horse beerhouse in the Beast Market, where their fifth child, Beatrice Alice, was born on September 9th 1887.

With Greenwood's rheumatism getting worse, he had to leave the running of the pub to his wife, Alice Ann, and she was once again helped by his mother and father. Greenwood finally became bedridden in the October of 1888, and the only time he got out of bed was the day the town was abuzz with the news of Billy Bates's attempted suicide.

Sadly, less than a month later, it was announced that Andrew Greenwood had died at the aged of 41, on February 12th 1889. He was buried on February 15th 1889 at Kirkheaton Graveyard. His grave is marked with a large stone headstone carved with a bat, gloves, pads and a ball breaking the wickets.

Allen Hill

Allen Hill was born on November 15th 1843 at New Town, Heaton (Kirkheaton), according to his baptism; but most of the other records have his birth as November 14th. He was baptised at Kirkheaton Parish Church on May 21st 1845. He was the ninth child of Francis (Frank) and Elizabeth (Betty) Hill (née Thornton), who were married at Kirkheaton Parish Church on September 6th 1825. He had six brothers: Thomas Thornton, born in 1825; William, born in 1826; Ephraim, born in 1828; Beaumont, born in 1830; Michael, born in 1834; and David, born in 1835. There were two sisters: Mary Ann, born in 1832; and Hannah, born in 1837. Sadly, Mary Ann died in her infancy.

Hill started to train to be a hand-loom weaver at an early age. He was introduced to the game of cricket by his brothers, who had him fielding the ball for them when they were practising, and sometimes when they were tired of bowling they would let him have a bowl at them. With the help of the Greenwood and Thewlis families (who lived nearby), Hill soon got quite good at the game.

He was encouraged to join them at the Lascelles Hall cricket club, but his first professional engagement was with Dewsbury in about 1860. It was for 3 matches and he was paid 5s (25p) per match. He later recalled in the *Yorkshire Evening Post*'s, 'Talks With Old Cricketers' how delighted his father and mother were when he showed them the 15s (75p). (A dozen bottles of claret was 20s (£1) and a dozen bottles of champagne was 32s (£1.60).) After the three games the Mirfield Old Club approached him, and they engaged him to play for them for 15s (75p) per week. That was short-lived, however, and he soon went back to being a hand-loom weaver.

A year after the death of his father, Frank, who died at the age of 62 in March 1863, he was recommended by Luke Greenwood for the post of coach and groundsman to Stoneyhurst College.

The college engaged Hill in the spring of 1864 and he stopped there for two years, but during his time with the college his mother, Betty, sadly died in January 1965 at the age of 61. Hill left Stoneyhurst College to become the groundsman at Old Trafford, and from there he went to Burnley.

Despite being employed in Lancashire, Hill still managed to spend a lot of time back home in Kirkheaton and Lascelles Hall, visiting family and friends, and on June 22nd 1868 he married Ellen Jessop at Kirkheaton Parish Church. Their first child – a son, Frank – was born on July 30th 1868, at Kirkheaton, and they moved to Common End, Lascelles Hall, which was next door to Ephraim Lockwood.

Yorkshire gave him the opportunity to show them what he could do in a match against the MCC at Lord's on May 22nd 1871, but he only got two wickets in the match (one in each innings), and he also got two ducks with the bat. Hill was also taught by C. Ullathorne that stupidity has to be paid for.

Young cricketers on going to town soon found themselves victims to those who knew their way about. Allan Hill once found this out. Andrew Greenwood, Allan and I were coming from Lord's, when Andrew said he wanted a shave. So did Allan and myself; so finally I said I would stand a glass of bitter each if Allan would stand the shaves. Allan was quite agreeable. The beers cost me 6d. At the barbers, Allen Hill was flabbergasted by the request made by the young lady at the counter, 'Three shaves, sir; 1s 6d, please.' He paid; and looked daggers at Andrew and I for an hour afterwards.

Yorkshire Evening Post
April 1st 1899

Not long after his return from London, the Hills' second child, Alice, was born on June 22nd 1871.

Hill had to wait until nearly the end of the season to get the chance to play in his first county match for Yorkshire. This was against Surrey at the Oval, on August 21st. Here he made more of his opportunity, as he and T. Emmett were bowled unchanged in both the Surrey innings. Hill was the better of the bowlers on this occasion, taking 12 wickets in his 50 overs for 56 runs, every one of them bowled (6 for 33 and 6 for 23); and he also made 28 with the bat. After the match he was presented with a silver cup in honour of his bowling. Hill later recalled his debut in the 'Talks With Old Cricketers' article.

Roger Iddison was the captain of Yorkshire at the time, and he wrote to me at Burnley to hurry up for the match, giving me instructions how to get to London, and what to do when I got there. George Freeman had broken down. Surrey had lost five of the six previous matches in succession to Yorkshire, the sixth being drawn. In the absence of the great Malton bowler they thought their turn had come, and they did not anticipate much damage from your humble servant.

Well, Surrey batted first, and Tom Emmett and I opened the Yorkshire bowling. You may be sure I was on my mettle, and I bowled my fastest and straightest. The result was that I clean bowled R. Humphrey, H.H. Stephenson, Mr. J.G. Gregory, W.H. Anstead, A. Freeman and Martin. My analysis for the innings was the following:

27 overs, 11 maidens, 33 runs, 6 wickets.

Tom Emmett took four wickets for 83 runs; and bowled the usual wide. Surrey were out for 111, but we did not come up to expectations with the bat, our figures being 100, towards which I was the chief contributor with 28. On going in a second time, Surrey did worse than before, and I think I must have bowled even better, some of the batsmen being clean beaten with the pace and length of the deliveries. I clean bowled R. and T. Humphrey, E. Pooley, Stephenson, Mr. W.H. Game, and Southerton, the analysis this time being:

23 overs, 8 maidens, 23 runs, 6 wickets.

Luke Greenwood and Joe Rowbotham afterwards knocked off the runs required, and we won by 10 wickets. You will see that I got 12 wickets for 56 runs. I had a silver cup given to me for the bowling performance. I went as a raw colt, and the Surreyites were naturally a bit astonished. I remember their wicketkeeper, H.H. Stephenson, had scarcely a pleasant experience. He had one ball in each innings: the second time he shook his bat at me and said as he walked away, 'You young —, you bowled me out before I was ready!' He often referred to the incident good-temperedly afterwards.

The Yorkshire Evening Post
December 11th 1897

This prompted Yorkshire to give him a regular place in the side, and the only place this news was not received well was at Burnley, because they had to try to find a replacement for him. Hill played in ten county matches for Yorkshire in the 1872 season, and he finished the season with 31 wickets for 545 runs.

Hill's career really took off in the 1873 season. He was now Yorkshire's top wicket taker, with 82 wickets for only 994 runs, giving him an average of 12.12, which meant he was also top of the bowling averages for Yorkshire.

Hill had a good start to the 1874 season, and it was Surrey that were made to suffer again. This time it was at Brammall Lane, Sheffield, on June 15th. He took 11 wickets for 121 runs (4 for 59 and 7 for 62) (9 of them bowled). Then, against the United South at Bradford on June 22nd, he took 9 wickets for 67 runs (3 for 58 and 6 for 9); this also included Hill's first hat-trick for Yorkshire. It was in the second innings and it managed to get the following report:

Hill bowled Charlwood with the next last ball of the over; Fillery fell next with the last ball of the over and with the first ball of the next over Phillips went, thereby gaining the new hat which is customarily presented when a bowler obtains a wicket from each three successive balls, and much laughter and applause amongst the spectators was caused when an officious member of the Bradford Cricket Club appeared with a new tile in his hand and crowned Allen with it upon the field. Hills' bowling was something to be wondered at.

Huddersfield Daily Examiner
June 25th 1874

Hill was picked to play for the Players against the Gentlemen, and in the second of the matches, at Lord's on July 6th 1874, Hill became the first player to take a hat-trick in such games, which also got him a mention in the press.

It was a disastrous beginning for the Gentlemen, Mr. Walker's leg stump being bowled by the second ball of Hill's over. From that which followed Mr. Ridley was caught and bowled, while from the last ball of the fatal over

Unfortunately, Hill's season was cut short when he was injured while playing for Yorkshire against Gloucestershire at Brammall Lane, Sheffield, on July 29th 1874 (Luke Greenwood's benefit match). He had to leave the field on the first day, and he was unable play for Yorkshire for the rest of the season. Hill still finished the season with 45 wickets for 482 runs from the 6 matches he played for Yorkshire.

Hill was able to play in Yorkshire's first match of the 1875 season, which was against Middlesex at the Prince's ground on May 20th. By the time of the return match came round, which was at Brammall Lane, Sheffield, on August 9th, Hill was getting his form back and he took 10 wickets for 66 runs (6-34 and 4-32). He finished the season with 58 wickets for 827 runs.

Hill's son, Frank, sadly died in January 1876, but they had a third child, Lilly, on June 1st 1876, at Lascelles Hall. Despite the ups and downs at the beginning of the year, Hill still managed to have a good season with the ball. He took 9 wickets for 62 runs (6-24 and 3-38) against Lancashire at Old Trafford on June 22nd. He also made them suffer in the return match at Brammall Lane, Sheffield, on July 10th, taking 8 wickets for 50 runs (2-22 and 6-28). He finished top of the Yorkshire bowling averages with an average of 10.44, taking 55 wickets for 574 runs from the 10 matches he played in.

At the end of the 1876 season Hill accepted an invitation to go on Lillywhite's (1876-77) tour of Australia, along with fellow Lascelles Hall and Yorkshire player A. Greenwood and fellow Yorkshire players T. Armitage, T. Emmett and G. Ulyett. Hill had a good tour and he took 113 wickets in all matches, but the most important of those wickets was towards the end of the tour.

When the England XI played the Combined Melbourne and Sydney XI at the Melbourne Cricket ground on March 15th 1877

– which is now regarded as the first Test match in cricket – Australia won the toss and decided to bat. Shaw opened the bowling for England, with Hill bowling at the other end, and when Hill dislodged the bails of Thompson, he became the first bowler to take a wicket in a Test match. A little later on in the match he caught Blackham off the bowling of Shaw, and thus he became the first man to take a catch in a Test match. He finished the match with 2 wickets for 60 (1 for 42 and 1 for 18) and he scored 35 runs not out in the first innings. He was duly promoted to open the second innings for England but this time got a duck.

When he returned from the tour, Hill was due to play in Yorkshire's second county match of the season, which was against Surrey at Sheffield on June 18th 1877, but his county return had to be postponed due the death of his youngest daughter, Lilly, on June 17th 1877. His first county match of the season was therefore against Nottinghamshire at Trent Bridge, Nottingham, on June 25th. The season wasn't a good one for Hill; he only took 21 wickets for 409 runs.

Midway through the 1878 season, the Hills had a fourth child, Cathrine May, who was born at Shop Lane, Kirkheaton on July 20th. It was also another relatively poor season for Hill, only taking 29 wickets for 403 runs.

The 1879 season went better for Hill. He took 9 wickets for 25 runs (5-15 and 4-9) against Derbyshire at Brammall Lane, Sheffield, on July 14th. He got his best figures in an innings for Yorkshire, taking 7 wickets for 14 runs, in the first innings against Surrey at Hull on June 12th, but play was cut short and he didn't get another chance to bowl in the match. Due to illness, Hill's 1879 season had to be curtailed. Again, he only managed to play in 6 matches, but he still finished the season with 29 wickets for 193 runs and he was top of the bowling averages for Yorkshire with an average of 6.19.

Hill was trying to get ready to bounce back for Yorkshire in the 1880 season, when his fifth child, Gertrude, was born on May 7th at Kirkheaton. He was back in full swing by the time Yorkshire played Derbyshire at the Saint John's Ground, Huddersfield, on July 22nd, taking 7 wickets for 82 runs (2-58 and 5-24). He also had another good game against Surrey at the

Oval on August 12th, taking 8 wickets for 50 runs (2-24 and 6-26), which included another hat-trick, which got the subdued write-up of, 'Hill bowled well and took a hat-trick.'

Hill was bowling well at the beginning of the 1881 season, taking 23 wickets for 264 runs by the end of June. He went down to London to play in the Gentlemen against Players matches, but the wickets didn't suit his bowling and he was let go after the first of the matches at the Oval on July 1st. Hill was unable to get to Yorkshire's next county match, (which was against Lancashire), and with Yorkshire due to play Kent at Maidstone on July 21st. He decided to stop in the South and play in a couple of matches for the United XI of England.

The matches were in the Birmingham area and everything started well for Hill. He took 23 wickets against the Nuneaton and District XXII on July 7th 1881. But everything went wrong for Hill when they played against XVI of the Edgbaston Club at the Lower Ground, Aston, on July 11th. Hill went into bat late on in the first day and he had an accident and broke his collarbone.

A. Hill was the newcomer, but in making a run he cannoned against the wicketkeeper, and both fell, Hill breaking his collarbone.

The Birmingham Daily Post
July 12th 1881

Hill managed to make yet another comeback in he 1882, playing in most of Yorkshire's matches that season. But his shoulder was not as strong as it was, and he wasn't as accurate as he was before the accident, and he only picked up 22 wickets for an average of 19.27.

The following season, Yorkshire only picked Hill for two matches, and that was only because Yorkshire had several players unable to play for them. By chance, both the games were against Leicestershire. The first was at Leicester on June 21st 1883, and he took 7 wickets (5 and 2). The second was at Brammall Lane on July 9th, and he took 8 wickets for 41 runs (6-18 and 2-23); he also made 33 runs with the bat. They had a sixth child, Mabel, on July 14th 1883. At the end of the season, Hill decided it was time to finish playing first class cricket.

Hill's Career Figures:

Batting
County Runs	1,786
Average	8.79
Test Runs	101
Average	50.50

Bowling
County Wickets	563
Runs	7,151
Average	12.70
Test Wickets	7
Runs	130
Average	18.57

Others
County Catches	91
Test Catches	1

After he retired, Hill was asked to be the groundsman at Old Trafford again. Yorkshire also held a benefit match for him on July 16th 1884; it was against Lancashire at Brammall Lane, Sheffield; it raised £376. (Butter was then 1s (5p) per lb. and flour was 1s 7d (8p) per stone.)

After the death of his wife, Ellen, at the age of 41 on December 28th 1889, Hill was asked to be the coach and groundsman of the Leyland cricket club by Mr. John Stanning. He was a noted cricket enthusiast who tried his best to help retired cricketers from falling on hard times after their career was over, by providing them suitable employment and affordable lodgings. So Hill moved the family to Leyland in Lancashire.

Hill's daughter, Alice, married William Hogarth at St Andrew's, Leyland in 1892. Hill married Margaret Whittle in 1900.

Allen Hill died in Leyland at the age of 64, on August 28th 1910. He was buried at St Andrew's, Leyland; the grave is marked with a simple marble headstone.

Edward Lumb

Edward Lumb was born at Colne Road, Huddersfield, on September 12th 1852, and baptised at Kirkheaton Parish Church on April 19th 1857; he was the seventh child of Joseph and Elizabeth Lumb (née Wrathful). They were married at Kirkheaton Parish Church on February 25th 1838. He had four brothers: William, born in 1844; Jesse, born in 1846; Edwin, born in 1848; and Joah, born in 1851. There were four sisters: Sarah Ann, born in 1838; Mary, born in 1839; Elizabeth; born in 1842; and Jane, born in 1856. Sadly for the family, Edwin died at the age of three in May 1852, which was just four months before Edward was born.

Lumb's father, Joseph, started out as a farmer at Gregory, Whitley, but in about 1845, he and his brother started a spinning and weaving firm at Aspley. Joseph moved the family to Kilner Bank, Dalton, which was closer to the Aspley mill, they then moved to Colne Road about twelve months before Edward was born. Around 1853 Joseph Lumb decided to go it alone and he moved the spinning part of the mill to Folly Hall, Colne Bridge and the family move to Stables Street, Colne Bridge.

Although the spinning mill became a success, it was hard work in the beginning, and all the family had to help out to make it thrive. Edward and William were wool-sorters, Joah was a packer and Jesse was an overlooker. His sisters also did their bit; his eldest sister, Sarah, was a housekeeper, and Mary and Elizabeth were dressmakers.

Lumb started playing cricket at an early age, along with his brother Joah, for the Standard club, which was based at Deadwaters, and he was soon described as a good cricketer. The Standard Club moved to Primrose Hill, and Lumb started to lose interest, and in about 1869 he and his brother moved to the Dalton cricket club, which was then based just out of town centre at Carr Pit.

At the end of the 1870 season Lumb was asked to play for the Yorkshire Colts against the United North at Grimston Park, Tadcaster, on September 9th 1870. However, he didn't play too well, only scoring 11 runs in the first innings, and getting a duck in the second.

Lumb was gaining the respect of some of the senior players for his knowledge of the game, and he was made the captain of the Dalton club in 1871. One of the players, Tom Ramsden, was often heard saying, 'Lumb had the clearest head on cricket matters he ever knew.'

Lumb was asked to play for the Colts of England against the United North at the Savile ground, Dewsbury, on May 20th 1872. He got a duck in the first innings and he was thrown out for 17 runs in the second. But less than a month before his twentieth birthday, Lumb got his first opportunity to play in a county match for Yorkshire. This was against Gloucestershire at Brammall Lane, Sheffield, on July 29th 1872; but unfortunately for Lumb, W.G. Grace was at the top of his game, and Grace took his wicket in the first innings for a duck. He didn't fare any better in the second either. Lumb did get a bit of revenge after the match, though:

Mr. W.G. Grace went to the wicket when the match was concluded, to delight the spectators by a further exhibition of his splendid batting, but he was caught by Lumb when he had scored two.

Huddersfield Weekly Examiner
August 3rd 1872

Lumb was on the fringes of the Yorkshire team in the 1873 season and he was also invited to play for the North of England against Elland at Elland on April 14th 1873. But he had got more involved in the family business, taking over as the buyer, which meant he had to spend a lot of time away, which left him less time to practise. The business was going from strength to strength, and the family moved to Gledholt Grove, Greenhead Road, which was a more affluent part of Huddersfield.

Lumb started channelling a lot of his energy into the Dalton cricket club, and in 1875 he and fellow members spent a lot of time getting the new ground at Kilner Bank, Dalton, ready for the start of the 1876 season. This involved trying to level the ground as much as possible, and removing stones from the playing area. With money on the tight side, they had to reuse most of the stones to build the boundary wall. It took considerable effort, but as described in the press it was completed on time.

The greater portion of the work has been done by voluntary labour, and when we say that in some places between four and five feet of stuff had to be taken off, and in others from five to eight feet put on, it will admitted at once that if the members had not been very sanguine they would never have attempted to make a cricket field out of the unpromising piece of ground at Hill Top. At one corner of the field a new brick tent is being erected, about fourteen yards long, and from the side of this is one of the best, if not the best views of Huddersfield, may be obtained, and we have no doubt many besides admirers of cricket will occasionally take a walk up there and enjoy the splendid view of the surrounding country which it affords.

Huddersfield Weekly Examiner
April 15th 1876

With the new ground ready, Lumb could once again concentrate on his cricket. He was playing well, and at the end of the 1876 season he was picked for the Yorkshire Gents and Players against Lascelles Hall on September 1st 1876. He managed to score 23 runs and 32 not out.

Lumb was picked for the Yorkshire County XI against Wakefield and District at the College ground Wakefield, on June 14th 1877, and he showed them what he could do with the bat. He was the top scorer in the first innings with 57 runs, and he was 22 not out in the second. He was then picked for the North against the South at Hull on July 23rd 1877, and scored 30 runs.

At the beginning of the 1878 season he was picked for the Gentlemen of England against the Players of the North at Dewsbury, on May 16th 1878, but only scored 8 not out and 3 runs. He was then picked for Yorkshire against Australia at the Athletic Ground, Fartown, Huddersfield, on May 29th 1878. Here he again failed to show his full potential, only scoring 10 runs and 3 runs. Yorkshire again overlooked him for a county match in the 1878 season.

Lumb's father, Joseph, sadly died at the age of 68 in the April of 1879, which meant Edward had to spend more time helping his brothers run the family firm, but he still managed to find time to play for the local teams.

Lumb was having a good 1881 season with the bat, and when he turned out for the Liberals in a benefit match for the Huddersfield Infirmary at Fartown on July 20th 1881, he delighted the crowd with a fine display in the art of batting, and at the end of play he was 161 not out. Lumb was then asked to play for Lascelles Hall, in a benefit match for A. Hill against a Yorkshire XI at the Savile ground, Dewsbury, on August 5th. He and W. Bates opened both the innings for Lascelles Hall. He scored 9 runs in the first innings, and in the second innings his was the last wicket to fall for Lascelles Hall and he was the top scorer with 50 runs. Unfortunately he was hit on the chest by a ball, which fractured one of his ribs. This didn't stop him, and he still turned out for Huddersfield's next match on August 10th 1881, and he made 115 not out.

Lumb must have thought he was destined never to play another county match for Yorkshire.

The weavers went on strike in 1883, and this meant Lumb was able to spend a lot more time on the cricket field. Lumb's form was brought to the attention of Yorkshire, and he was picked to play against Leicestershire at Sheffield on July 12th 1883. He opened the innings and he was left there on 82 not out at the close of the innings, which only got him a few words in the papers.

The Yorkshire innings closed for 183, Lumb bringing out his bat for a faultless 82.

Huddersfield Weekly Examiner
July 14th 1883

Lumb stayed in Sheffield and he was picked to play in Yorkshire's next match, which was against Lancashire on July 16th 1883. He only scored 4 runs in the first innings and 8 not out in the second innings; Yorkshire won the match by 8 wickets. He was then included in Yorkshire's team for the match against Surrey at the Oval on July 26th 1883. He acquitted himself a bit better this time, scoring 12 runs and 60 not out in the second. Lumb still had no answer to W.G. Grace at Horton Park Avenue, Bradford, on July 30th 1883 with W.G. taking his wicket twice for 4 runs and 3 runs. Lumb's best performance came in the last match of the season, which was against Middlesex at Fartown on August 23rd. Middlesex were unable to get him out, and he was the top scorer with 70 not out in the first innings and he followed it up with 24 not out. After the match he was presented with a silver cup worth £10. (Fancy silk was then 1s 11d (9½ p) per yard, and rent for a two-bedroom house in Portland Street was £12 per annum.) This time his efforts got a few more words in the papers.

At the close of this match on Saturday, a silver cup, value £10, was presented to Mr. Lumb for his fine play throughout the match, but particularly in the first innings of Yorkshire, in which he batted so well that he saved the eleven from having to follow on.

Huddersfield Weekly Examiner
September 1st 1883

At the end of the season Lumb was second in the Yorkshire batting averages.

With the cloth industry getting back to normal in 1884, Lumb had to concentrate on the family business, which meant he missed most of the 1884 season.

He started playing in local cricket again in the 1885 season, and he even got the chance to team up with his old Yorkshire team-mate, E. Lockwood, when Lockwood signed for Dalton. Towards the end of the season Lumb was picked to play for the Yorkshire Gentlemen against the Yorkshire Players at York on August 7th 1885, but he only got 8 runs and a duck.

In the spring of 1886 the local press started to get behind the region's cricket, and a cricket association was formed; but the press still weren't satisfied and suggested that a Challenge Cup should be played for.

There is one matter, which might very well be taken up by some of our leading clubs. Why should not Huddersfield have a Cricket Challenge cup?

Huddersfield Weekly Examiner
April 3rd 1886

As the 1886 season got under way, Lumb was again playing well for local cricket sides, and this got him recalled to the Yorkshire side for their match against the Midlands Counties at Birmingham on July 19th. He scored 32 runs in the first innings and he didn't get the chance to bat in the second. He was picked to play against Lancashire at Savile Town, Dewsbury, on July 29th, but he failed yet again to convert his local cricket form to the county game, only scoring 8 runs and getting a duck in the second. His last county match for Yorkshire was against Kent at Canterbury, on August 5th 1886 and he only scored 5 runs and 8 runs. At the end of the season he decided to dedicate his time to work and local cricket.

LUMB'S CAREER FIGURES:

Batting

Runs	489
Average	21.26

Others

Catches	5

At the inaugural Huddersfield and District Cricket Association dinner at the Queen's Hotel on November 6th 1886, Lumb announced he was to sponsor a Challenge Cup, which was to be first played for in the 1887 season. Lumb was very much anti-professionalism, so he set the cup with strict rules, and one of the strictest was that the cup was for amateurs only and the clubs had to rest their professionals for the cup games.

The first match for the Lumb Cup was between Delph and Rastrick at Delph on May 7th 1887, with Delph winning.

The first final was played at Lockwood on August 20th the same year, and it was between Armitage Bridge and Lascelles Hall; but Lascelles Hall lacked their professional players and Armitage Bridge won the match easily. The £61 9s 6d (£61.47½) gate money was donated to the Huddersfield Royal Infirmary. (Cane granulated sugar was 2d (0.75p) per lb.; finest lump sugar was 2¼d (0.82p) per lb. It cost 6d (2½p) or 1s (5p) to see Yorkshire play Middlesex at Fartown, and a restorer of grey hair cost 1s (5p) per bottle.)

Lumb had to spend a lot more time away on company business, which meant he had a lot less time to play cricket, but most of his spare time was spent playing the game he loved. He was also a good advocate of the game and he often spoke out against the effect gambling was having on cricket and also about the growth in professionalism affecting the loyalty of some of the players. His belief was you should play just for the love of it.

Shortly after the death of his mother Elizabeth at the age of 75, in December 1890, Lumb went on his usual business trip to the London wool sales. He set off to London with a slight cold; unfortunately, the cold got worse and it turned into pleurisy. Sadly, Edward Lumb died at the Hotel Metropole, London, at the age of 38 on April 5th 1891. His body was brought back to Huddersfield and he was buried in the family vault in Edgerton Cemetery on April 9th.

His ideals regarding the game were soon forgotten, and even Dalton – the club he spent so much time and energy on – started asking for a change in the rules of the Lumb Cup, to allow the use of professional players in cup matches.

Billy Bates

Billy (registered as Willie) Bates was born at Waterloo, Huddersfield, on November 19th 1855. He was the fifth child of John William and Mary Bates (née Kay). His father was a tailor, and they were married at Kirkheaton Parish Church on April 14th 1846. He was baptised at Kirkheaton Parish Church on February 1st 1869. He had five brothers: Henry, born in 1846; William, born in 1852; Fred, born in 1858; George, born in 1860; and Harry, born in 1864. He had three sisters: Hannah, born in 1849; Mary Ann, born in 1853; and Alice, born in 1866. Henry and William died within four months of each other in 1852, and were buried at Kirkheaton graveyard.

Bates grew up in the Cowms and Tandem area of Lepton, and he was only young when the family started struggling to make ends meet, so his father became a journeyman tailor. This meant his father had to spend long periods of time from home, and they just managed to keep out of the workhouse on several occasions. Despite this Billy still managed to find time to play cricket with Lascelles Hall, which was now being called 'the Yorkshire nursery'.

To help with the family budget, Billy became a trainee hand-loom weaver, but at the age of seventeen Bates decided to accept an offer to be a professional with the Rochdale cricket club. Bates must have questioned his decision to turn professional when his father died at the beginning of July 1876 at the age of 53.

Bates stuck by his decision and he made his county debut for Yorkshire against Middlesex at Lord's on June 4th 1877. In the first innings he was run out for 3 runs, but he managed to take 4 wickets, and in the second he got 12 runs and took just 1 wicket. Bates went on to finish his first season with 127 runs and he only took 8 wickets for 207 runs.

The following season Bates got the first of his nine centuries (102), which was against Nottingham at Brammall Lane, Sheffield, on June 24th 1878, and he also took 7 wickets for 75 runs (2-58 and 5-17). He got all the acclaim when Yorkshire played Gloucestershire at Brammall Lane, on July 29th, for taking 11 wickets for 102 runs (4-64 and 7-38) and he even managed to claim the wicket of W.G. Grace, he was also 38 not out in the second innings.

Bates bowled magnificently, and received a splendid ovation when he cleaned bowled the champion.

Huddersfield Daily Examiner
August 3rd 1878

Bates lifted the spirits of a wet Huddersfield crowd in a weather-affected match against Lancashire at the Saint John's ground, Huddersfield, on August 8th 1878, by taking 8 wickets for 45 runs in their first and only innings. He also took 9 wickets for 26 runs (7-19 and 2-7), against Sussex at Brighton on August 12th 1878. He finished the season with an average of 17.2 with the bat, and he was top of the Yorkshire bowling averages, taking 71 wickets for 845 runs at an average of 11.9.

Bates was fast getting a reputation for his all-round ability on the field and for being a bit of a dandy off the field, so he was given the nickname of 'the Duke'.

Bates started the 1879 season a bit slowly, but he and E. Peate managed to pull off a remarkable victory for Yorkshire against Gloucestershire at Sheffield on July 28th 1879. Bates took 6 wickets for 72 runs (2-60 and 4-12), with his bowling in the second innings getting the acclaim.

There was a perfect Babel of noise – hats, sticks, and umbrellas going up in the air – when Miles played one which appeared to be going back to Peate, but Emmett rushed in from mid off and snapped the ball before it had a chance of reaching him, and Yorkshire thus achieved one of the most glorious victories ever yet won by them. The bowling of Peate and Bates was an especial feature of the match, Bates's being an especially brilliant performance.

Huddersfield Weekly Examiner
August 2nd 1879

But T. Emmett later recalled the match for another reason, which cost him 50 shillings or £2.50. (Bacon was 8d (3½p) per lb.; ham was 9d (4p) per lb., and an excursion from Lockwood to Liverpool by train was 3s (15p) return.)

I must tell you of a remarkable match we had at Sheffield Yorkshire v Gloucestershire on July 28, 29 and 30 1879, when I lost a fancy bet of 50s to 1s. Gloucestershire made 253 runs in the first innings against 128 and 195, and on going in a second time they only wanted 71 runs to win. At lunch time they had scored 34 for 2 wickets, so that with 8 wickets to go down they only needed 27 runs. Those 8 wickets moreover included W.G., G.F. and E.M. Grace. Going to luncheon with Bates, I made a remark about it being Windsor Castle to a Guinea Gloucestershire winning. 'What odds will you lay, Tom?' asked Bates. 'Fifty to one on,' was my rash reply. Bates handed me a shilling and took the odds. An hour and a half or so afterwards I had 51s to pay. Yorkshire won the match by seven runs.

Yorkshire Evening Post
January 22nd 1898

Bates thrilled his home crowd again when Yorkshire played Middlesex at the Saint John's ground, Huddersfield, on August 7th 1879. He took 9 wickets for 55 runs (3-44 and 6-11). In Yorkshire's next match, Bates got another century (118), which was against Lancashire at Brammall Lane, Sheffield, on August 11th. Two weeks later against Surrey at the Oval on August 25th Bates got his best bowling figures in an innings, taking 8 wickets for 21 runs, in the first and only innings. At the end of the season Bates was second in both the batting and bowling averages for Yorkshire.

Bates started the 1880 season a bit better, and not even his 11 wickets for 67 runs (6-34 and 5-33) could stop Yorkshire losing to Nottinghamshire at Trent Bridge, Nottingham, on June 28th. Bates was picked for the Players against the Gentlemen, and he was the top scorer, with 87 in the second match at Lord's on July 8th. He then took 10 wickets for 68 runs for Yorkshire against Nottinghamshire at Brammall Lane, Sheffield, on August 9th. He finished the 1880 season with 56 wickets for 735 runs from his 12 matches for Yorkshire, but he had a poor season with the bat, only scoring 306 runs.

Just before the start of the 1881 season Bates married Sarah

Elizabeth Medley at Kirkheaton Parish Church on May 25th 1881. With A. Hill and E. Lockwood being witnesses they could have had a quick practice match instead of a reception after the wedding!

Bates had a good start to the 1881 season, taking 6 wickets for 22 runs in the first innings against Kent at Bradford on June 13th, and he also took 11 wickets for 47 runs (5-30 and 6-17) against Nottinghamshire at Trent Bridge, Nottingham on June 27th. Bates was even in a bit of form with the bat and he got 108 out of 135 against Kent at Maidstone on July 21st, hitting 1 six and 18 fours. He finished the season with 528 runs and he was Yorkshire's second top wicket-taker with 72 wickets for 1,090 runs.

Bates was invited on the 1881-82 tour of the Antipodes with Shaw's England XI, and E. Peate recalled how Bates and the team became acquainted with King Kalakaua of the Sandwich Islands. It seems the King even asked them to play an unscheduled game at Honolulu:

> On our voyage from San Francisco to Australia we enjoyed the distinguished company of the King of the Sandwich Islands, King Kalakaua, as far as the islands. King Kalakaua called us into his cabin on board the Australia (the ship we sailed in) every morning in order to hear Billy Bates sing 'The Bonny Yorkshire Lass'.
>
> At Honolulu we had an invitation to the King's Palace. The King offered our ship's captain £300 if he would wait until we could play a match, but though Shaw and Lillywhite were quite prepared to play a game to please his highness, the captain would not accept the offer. He could have done so as he was in front of time then; in fact he beat the record from 'Frisco to Sydney by two days.

Yorkshire Evening Post
April 2nd 1898

Bates played his first Test match on the tour, which was at Melbourne on December 31st 1881. He got 58 runs in the first innings and he took 2 wickets for 43 runs; in the second innings he scored 47 runs and took 2 wickets for 43 runs again. Bates finished his Test series with 192 runs, and 16 wickets for 334 runs.

When he returned to England, Bates got no time to rest, going straight from the ship to play for Yorkshire in the pre-season warm-up games. When the season started, he took 9 wickets for 53 runs (3-22 and 6-31) and he also scored 54 in the first innings for Yorkshire against Derbyshire at Saint John's ground, Huddersfield, on June 1st 1882. Then against Kent at Brammall Lane, Sheffield, on June 12th, Bates took 9 wickets for 59 runs (3-47 and 6-12), he and E. Peate bowling Kent out in the second innings for 39 runs.

Bates was not picked for the fateful Test match in 1882, but he was picked to go on the Honourable Ivo Bligh's tour of Australia in the winter of 1882-83.

Unfortunately, Bates's older sister, Mary Ann, died just before they set sail.

Fortunately for England, Bates still went on the tour and in the second Test at Melbourne on January 19th 1883, Bates's name was consigned to the record books. In Australia's first innings Bates took the first hat-trick by a bowler in Test cricket, and he finished the innings with 7 wickets for 28 runs. He then went on to score 55 runs in the England innings. In the second innings, according to the Wisden, he took 7 wickets for 74 runs (but according to the report in one of the local papers it was 8 wickets for 74 runs). This made him the first cricketer to score 50 runs in an innings and take 10+ wickets in a match. He was also the first England bowler to take 5+ wickets in each innings, and take 10+ wickets in a Test match (the first to do these feats in a Test was Spofforth for Australia on the 1878-79 tour). This fine performance helped England win the game by an innings and 27 runs, which was the first time a Test match had been won by an innings; it was greeted back home with the following report.

> Indeed the fielding all round at this juncture was a treat to witness, and the rapidity with which the home wickets fell caused the local people to stand almost breathless with amazement. Bates's three successive balls having thus resulted with such deadly effect he was credited with the 'hat trick' for the first time in a first class match, and the performance elicited for him much congratulations.

Huddersfield Daily Examiner
March 7th 1883

In honour of this feat the Australians presented Bates with a mounted Ostrich egg, and after England won the third Test at Sydney, the captain was presented with the ashes of a burnt bail in a sealed urn in a red and gold embroidered bag.

Bates only managed to score 444 runs and take 40 wickets for 657 runs in the 1883 season. But he and Sarah had something to celebrate when their son, William Edrick, was born on March 5th 1884, at Tandem, Lepton.

Bates had another poor season in 1884, only taking 25 wickets for 564 runs and scoring 514 runs. Despite his poor year, Bates was still asked to go on the 1884-85 winter tour of Australia. Bates's form didn't improve much on the tour either.

The 1885 season started slowly for Bates, but he started to hit a bit of form in July, and against Surrey at Sheffield on July 25th he took 11 wickets for 68 runs (4-25 and 7-43). Then Bates delighted the Huddersfield crowd with a fine all-round performance against Lancashire on July 23rd, taking 7 wickets for 133 runs (6-85 and 1-48) and scoring 98 runs in Yorkshire's first innings. His 82 not out in the second innings helped Yorkshire to win the game.

> *Amidst tremendous cheers, Bates made the winning hit off the last ball of Yates's eight over a few minutes before 5.30. Included in Bates's dashing 82 were eleven 4s, four 3s and five 2s.*

Huddersfield Weekly Examiner
August 1st 1885

Bates seemed to becoming more of a batsman in the 1886 season; he got three centuries and Yorkshire started to pick him to open the innings. The first of his centuries was against Cheshire at Stockport on June 11th 1886. Bates still managed to do a bit with the ball too, picking up 6 wickets for 19 runs in the only innings of a rain-affected match against Lancashire at Savile Town, Dewsbury, July 29th. But it was the later part of the season when Bates got the second of the centuries, which was also his highest score in a county match. It was against Sussex at Brighton on August 23rd. In Yorkshire's second innings, Bates scored 136 runs out of a partnership of 186 runs. He had a bit of luck when he was dropped on 16 and then again on 71. He got the third of the centuries in another fine display of all-round cricket against Derbyshire at Holbeck on August 26th 1886. Here he scored 108 runs in the first innings, and he also took 10 wickets for 75 runs (5-30 and 5-45). He finished the season with 747 runs in county matches for Yorkshire, but he managed to score 1,093 in all matches in the season, which was the only time he got over 1,000 runs in a season.

Bates was again picked for the winter tour of Australia, but in the two Test matches he only managed 70 runs and only took 5 wickets for 53 runs.

When Bates returned to the Yorkshire team they were still picking him to open the innings, but the runs started to dry up. Bates was dropped down the order for Yorkshire's match against Derbyshire at Derby on June 25th 1887, and it seemed to work. He had a good game, scoring 103 runs and taking 8 wickets for 74 runs (4-42 and 4-32). It was only a one-off, and he finished the season with 594 runs and 29 wickets for 954 runs; despite this he was still picked for the 1887-88 tour of Australia.

On the Christmas Eve of 1887, the team was practising for the Boxing Day Test at Melbourne, when a ball came from the nets next to where Bates was practising and it struck him in the eye. The news soon got back to the English papers.

W. Bates, a member of Mr. Vernon's team, while practising here, has been struck in the eye by a ball. It is, however, hoped that his sight will be unimpaired.

Huddersfield Weekly Examiner
December 31st 1887

Bates was sent back to England just as soon as it was possible for him to go. The day after his return, the secretary of Surrey cricket club, Mr. Alcock, arranged for Bates to see the top ophthalmic surgeon, Dr. Critchett. This was on the Sunday, and it is said that it was the only time Dr. Critchett saw a patient on a Sunday. But the damage was irreparable, and Bates was forced to retire from first class cricket.

Bates's Career Figures:

Batting
County Runs	6,877
Average	20.90
Centuries	9
Test Runs	656
Average	27.33

Bowling
County Wickets	660
Runs	11,024
Average	16.70
Centuries	9
Test Wickets	50
Runs	821
Average	16.45

Others
County Catches	163
Test Catches	7

All Bates's Test matches were played in Australia, and out of the 15 matches he played in England won seven and two were drawn. After the accident the Australian people started a fund to raise money for the Yorkshireman they had taken to their hearts.

Bates put a lot of the money into a sports shop, but unfortunately it started to fail shortly after it opened, and he was still living the same lifestyle he had when he was earning money playing cricket. The injury was also causing Bates to suffer from depression, and this coupled with the failing of the shop drove Bates in desperation to try to take his own life on January 24th 1889. The story was reported with great relish by the press.

THE ATTEMPTED SUICIDE BY BATES, THE CRICKETER

We deeply regret to state that this morning, about nine o'clock, William Bates, of Little Carr Green, Dalton, in his day one of Yorkshire's most celebrated cricketers, made an attempt to commit suicide by cutting his throat with a razor, and he inflicted such injuries that life is despaired of.

He got up shortly before nine o'clock and came downstairs, and directly afterwards Mrs. Bates heard a curious noise which induced her to go downstairs, and there she found her husband laid on the floor, with a wound in his throat which had evidently been inflicted by a razor, which she found in the room. She immediately raised an alarm, and immediately sent for a Medical man. Dr. Barclay, of Moldgreen, was soon in attendance. The police were also informed of the occurrence, and Police-constable Oakes was soon in attendance, and set to watch over the patient, who is in a state of great prostration. Bates is receiving every attention, and we are sure the news of the attempt to shorten his existence will be received with every feeling of regret, as he was very popular as a cricketer.

Huddersfield Daily Examiner
January 24th 1889

After he had recovered enough, Bates was charged with attempting to commit suicide. He appeared at the Huddersfield Borough Police Court on February 25th 1889, and he pleaded guilty to the charge. It was reported in the papers the same day.

Mr. Ward, the chief constable, stated that on the 24 January last, the defendant, who was in a depressed state of mind consequent on business difficulties, attempted to take away his life. Since then he had been suffering from that attempt, and this was the first time he had been out since the occurrence. The doctor who had attended Bates would say that his state of mind during that time had been most depressed, and was so still, and he would require attention from his friends if the Bench adopt the course he (Mr. Ward) was about to suggest. Under the circumstances, seeing that Bates was in such a state of mind at the time as to be scarcely responsible for his act, and that no good could possibly accrue from continued prosecution of him, and with the hope that the result of his action would prevent Bates repeating the offence, he had to ask that the Bench would allow him to withdraw from the charge, and at the same time express hope that Bates would recover his mind and physical strength, and never again be found in a similar position.

Dr. Richardson, in reply to the Bench, stated that on the 24 January he saw Bates soon after the unfortunate affair happened, and found him suffering from a wound in the throat, coupled with very great loss of blood. He was now recovering from the wound, and also continued to improve in strength. He still remained very much depressed in mind, and his condition of mind before the accident led him to ask his friends to take very great precautions. He did not think there was any fear of Bates repeating the offence.

Mr. Ward said there was someone present to undertake to watch him.
Dr. Richardson said Bates's brother would do so. The Bench
discharged Bates, who went away with his wife and his brother George.

Huddersfield Daily Examiner
February 25th 1889

This desperate act stunned his friends and the Yorkshire Committee into action, and they opened a subscription fund for him, and with donations from all over the world it soon raised £1,000. But this time it was decided that the money would be invested for him, and the interest gave him an income of 8s 6d (42.5p) per week. He also received 6s (30p) from the professional cricketers' superannuation fund. (Rent for a three-bed house was £9 per year; tea was 1s (5p) 1s 4d (6.5p) or 1s 7d (8p) per lb., depending on the blend; Danish butter was 11d (4.5p) per lb., and Irish butter was 9d (4p) per lb.)

E. Lockwood had a good talk with Bates and he persuaded him to start playing sports again. Bates took Lockwood's advice and he became a good billiard player, which helped him earn a few extra shillings to make life a bit easier for him and his son. (It was said that he even did a bit of boxing and wrestling.)

Unfortunately, just as Bates was getting over the tragic incident, his wife, Sarah Elizabeth, died, at the young age of 28, on March 20th 1891. Once again Bates had to pick himself up. He started playing cricket again and he played alongside E. Lockwood when Lascelles Hall won the Heavy Woollen Cup in 1891.

Bates's interest in cricket was rekindled, and Leek cricket club signed him for the 1892 season. As the season was coming to a close it was reported that he had been signed as the coach of the Wanderers cricket club, Johannesburg, South Africa, at an annual fee of £300. (A three-bed front house was then 5s 3d (26p) per week; a four-room back house was 19s 9d (99p) per month; and a day return from Huddersfield to Hull was 3s (15p).) At the end of the season, Bates only had a couple of days in Huddersfield before he and his son had to set sail for South Africa, and they reached their destination at the end of November.

Bates still kept in touch with his old friends and when John Thewlis died he attended the funeral on January 1st 1900. At the funeral he and few of the other mourners caught a cold, but Bates's soon turned into pneumonia. A week after the funeral came the news that Billy Bates had died at the age of 44, on January 8th at Spa Bottom, Lascelles Hall. Bates was buried next to his wife in Kirkheaton Cemetery on January 11th 1900 (not next to Thewlis, as the popular legend has it). The grave is marked with a fairly simple headstone.

Bates's son, William Edrick, became a fair cricketer and he made his county debut for Yorkshire in 1907. He wasn't an all-rounder like his father but in his six years with Yorkshire he played in 113 county matches and scored 2,634 at an average of 17.33. With Billy Bates's nickname being 'the Duke', the wags in the changing room gave William Edrick the title of 'the Marquess'. William Edrick also had a stint with Glamorgan.

George Herbert Hirst

According to all the information I have been reading about George Herbert Hirst, he was born at the Brown Cow Inn, Saint Mary's, Kirkheaton, on September 7th 1871. He was the tenth child of James and Sarah Maria Hirst (née Woolhouse), who were married at Kirkheaton Parish Church on January 21st 1850. He had four brothers: Thomas, born in 1855; James, born in 1866; Job, born in 1868; and Henry, born in 1870. There were five sisters: Mary Elizabeth, born in 1847; Hannah, born in 1850; Sarah, born in 1851; Amelia, born in 1859; and Louisa, born in 1863; but Hannah died when she was one year old.

After the death of his father in the August of 1880, Hirst went to live with his sister, Mary Elizabeth, and her new husband, John Berry. They first lived at New Street, Kirkheaton, but they soon moved to Newtown, Kirkheaton.

Among their new neighbours were Allen Hill and his brother, William Hill, and the back of the houses would have been an ideal place for them to have a knockabout with a bat and ball. There was a long access road about ten feet wide, and with only a few small windows to the backs of the houses and a high wall at the other side. Hirst also spent a lot of time at the Brown Cow Inn, playing cricket in the yard with his brothers and friends. The inn backed onto the old Kirkheaton cricket ground and the players used to use it for their meetings.

After he left school, Hirst went to work at a local dying firm, and he was already making a name for himself as a good cricketer at Kirkheaton, and he was a major part of the Kirkheaton team that won the Lumb Challenge Cup final on August 3rd 1889. The game was watched by some of the Yorkshire players, and in a low scoring match, Hirst took 5 wickets for 23 runs. A few weeks later when Yorkshire played Cheshire at Fartown, Huddersfield, on August 9th, he was invited along with another local player to be part of the team. Hirst held his nerve; he started with a maiden, and finished the match with 3 wickets for 43 runs (3-35 and 0-8) He also scored 6 runs.

The following season he signed as the professional for Elland cricket club. Hirst was also picked to play in two of Yorkshire matches. The first was against Staffordshire at Stoke on June 6th 1890, but he didn't get the chance to play a big part in the match. He only took one wicket, he held onto one catch, but he didn't get the chance to bat. The second was against Essex at Leyton on June 28th, and he didn't show his true potential this time either. He got a duck in the first innings, he was 0 not out in the second, and he didn't have any luck with the ball either.

In the 1891 season, Hirst became the professional at the Mirfield cricket club. Yorkshire picked him for their match against Somerset at Taunton on July 23rd 1891. Again he failed to impose himself on the game as he only scored 15 runs (10 and 5), and took 2 wickets for 73 runs (0-41 and 2-32).

At the beginning of the 1892 season Hirst was picked by Yorkshire to play against the MCC at Lord's on May 16th. This time he managed to show them some of his potential. He took 6 wickets for 87 runs (4-29 and 2-58). He scored 20 runs in the first innings, and he was 43 not out in the second. This seems to be the turning point in Hirst's career. He was picked for the first home game of the season, which was against Essex at Dewsbury on May 19th. Then he was picked to play against Sussex at Sheffield on May 23rd, and in the second innings he took 6 wickets for 16 runs. He finished the season with 17 wickets for 346 runs.

Hirst's career was starting to take off, and in the 1893 season he took over 100 wickets (124) in a season for the first time.

At the beginning of the 1894 season, George Herbert started to endear himself into the hearts of the Yorkshire crowd, taking 10 wickets for 56 runs (7-25 and 3-31) against Lancashire in their own back yard at Manchester on May 14th.

Hirst was also instrumental in the Yorkshire match that started and finished on the same day; this was the first time Yorkshire had achieved this feat. The match was won by an innings and 5 runs at 6.25 p.m. It was against Somerset on July 19th 1894 in front of Hirst's home crowd at Fartown, Huddersfield. He took 5 wickets for 9 runs from 6.1 overs in the first innings; then he went out and scored 31 not out, and in the second innings he took 5 wickets for 44 runs from 17 overs. Towards the end of the season, against Gloucestershire at Bristol on August 20th, Hirst got 115 not out, which was the first of his 56 centuries for Yorkshire. Hirst finished the 1894 season by taking 7 wickets for 32 runs in the only innings in a rain-affected match against Somerset at Taunton on August 23rd.

Hirst's first hat-trick for Yorkshire was against Leicestershire at Leicester on June 6th 1895. The feat was simply recorded in the press: 'Hirst did the hat trick'. Hirst then took 7 wickets for 16 runs in the first innings against Essex at Harrogate on August 15th. Then, against Middlesex on a soft and treacherous Headingley pitch, he scored 29 not out in the first innings and took 12 wickets for 89 runs (6-49 and 6-40). He finished the 1895 season with 150 wickets.

Hirst married Emma Kilner at Kirkheaton Parish Church on January 1st 1896, and they moved to Square Hill, Kirkheaton. He celebrated by scoring over 1,000 runs in a season (1,145), and taking over 100 wickets, which meant he had achieved the double for the first time. The couple also had something else to celebrate when their first child, James, was born on October 6th that year.

Hirst was picked to play for the Players against the Gentlemen for the first time at the Oval on July 8th 1897. He scored 65 runs in the first and he was 4 not out in the second, even hitting the winning run, but he only took one wicket. In the second match at Lord's he scored 34 and 61 not out, but yet again he did nothing with ball.

Hirst was invited on the 1897-98 winter tour of Australia. His Test debut was at Sydney on December 13th 1897; he scored 62 runs and took 0 wickets for 106 runs. Hirst took his first Test wicket in the second Test at Melbourne. Hirst got his highest Test score of 85 runs in the third Test at Adelaide on January 14th 1898. The pitches didn't suit Hirst's style of bowling, and he only managed to take 2 wickets.

On his return, Hirst soon got among the runs for Yorkshire, scoring 130 not out, from a first innings total of 297, against Surrey at Bradford on June 6th 1898. It wasn't an over-impressive score for Hirst, but most of the runs came in a record-breaking ninth wicket stand for Yorkshire with S. Haigh. They put on 192, and this achievement even managed to get them a few words in the press.

As Hirst and Haigh had become partners at six o'clock on Tuesday with the score at 105, their partnership for the ninth wicket actually produced 192 runs in two hours and fifty minutes. At no time did the bowling, except occasionally that of Lockwood, cause them any serious difficulty. Haigh when 47 was nearly caught and bowled, Hirst when 47 was missed off one of Jephson's lobs from rather a difficult chance by Brockwell at deep square leg, but otherwise the batting was maintained at a high level of excellence. The wicket was still rather soft, but apart from Lockwood, none of the Surrey bowlers were able to make the ball turn. Haigh hit 9 fours, a three, and 9 twos. Admirably as he played, the great performance was that of Hirst, who going in at half past four on Tuesday when Yorkshire had lost four wickets for 44 runs, withstood the Surrey bowling for four hours and twenty minutes.

Huddersfield Weekly Examiner
June 11th 1898

During the 1899 season Hirst was picked to play in his first Test match in England, which was against Australia at Trent Bridge, Nottingham on June 1st; but again he failed to have an impact on the match, and he was dropped.

Hirst soon showed them what he was capable of when Yorkshire played Australia at Park Avenue, Bradford, on June 12th, taking 13 wickets for 149 runs (8-48 and 5-101). Towards the end of the season against Surrey at the Oval on August 10th 1899, Hirst set another Yorkshire record with the bat. This time it was for his fifth wicket stand with E. Wainwright. They put on 340 runs out of a Yorkshire total of 704. This time he got a few less words in the papers:

The chief cause of the performance was the extraordinary stand for the fifth wicket by Wainwright and Hirst. These professionals added 340 runs in three hours and forty minutes, and Wainwright's 228 and Hirst's 186 are both their highest compilations in first class cricket. Wainwright was missed three times, and hit 34 fours, 5 threes, and 22 twos. But Hirst's display was faultless, and included 31 fours, 2 threes, and 11 twos.

Huddersfield Weekly Examiner
August 12th 1899

At the end of the season Hirst had a batting average of 43.15, but his bowling was suffering, and he was fast becoming a batter who could bowl a bit.

During the close season the Hirsts moved to Field Place, Kirkheaton, and they had a second child, Annie, on December 5th 1899.

Again in the 1900 season, it was Hirst's batting that was the more dominant part of his playing, and he finished the season with a batting average of 42.43.

At the beginning of the 1901 season Hirst started to bounce back with the ball. He took 11 wickets for 82 runs (4-39 and 7-43) against Derbyshire at Huddersfield on May 20th. Then he took 13 wickets for 77 runs (5-54 and 7-23) against Lancashire at Manchester on May 27th; and 10 wickets for 114 (3-93 and 7-21) against Leicestershire at Scarborough on July 4th. Hirst didn't let his batting suffer; he got his first double century for Yorkshire, which was against Worcestershire at Worcester on July 11th. His 214 runs also took him over the 1,000 run mark for the season.

He finished the 1901 season just as strong with ball, taking 12 wickets for 29 runs (7-12 and 5-17) against Essex at Leyton on August 15th. He followed it up with 9 wickets for 102 runs (2-78 and 7-24) against Kent at Canterbury. At the end of the season Hirst was second in both the batting and bowling averages for Yorkshire.

In the 1902 season Hirst was recalled by England to play in the first Test against Australia at Edgbaston on May 29th. He had another mediocre game only scoring 48 runs and taking 3 wickets for 25 runs (3-15 and 0-10). Yet again, it was Yorkshire that got the best out of Hirst, and when they played Australia at Headingley on June 2nd 1902, he took 9 wickets for 44 runs (4-35 and 5-9). In the second innings the Australians were bowled out for 23 runs. Also, according to the report in the paper, Hirst just missed out on a hat-trick.

M.A. Noble had a swerve bowled by Hirst, played round and it hit the off stump. This was the first of Hirst's sixth over, and half the side was out for 20 runs. The holiday crowd shouted in exuberant glee and called to W. Armstrong to look out for the swerve; Armstrong guarded his off stump splendidly but the swerve carried the ball this time to the leg and the sixth Australian trailed his bat back to the pavilion. A.J. Hopkins arrived, and people were suddenly very quiet. Would Hirst perform the hat-trick? He

nearly did. He beat the batsman and the ball shaved past the leg stump.
But Hirst had already taken five wickets and it was destined that he should
have no more.

Huddersfield Daily Examiner
June 4th 1902

Hirst was dropped for the fourth Test, but he was recalled for the fifth at the Oval on August 11th 1902, and took 6 wickets for 84 runs (5-77 and 1-7). He had scored 43 runs in the first innings, and the Australians had their tails up in the second, when W. Rhodes joined him at the middle, and they managed to pull off a remarkable victory. England had just one wicket left and they still needed 15 runs for the victory; it is said Hirst just calmly walked up to Rhodes and said, 'Don't worry, we'll get these in singles.' They soon knocked off the runs and England won by one wicket.

Hirst was picked for the 1903-04 tour of Australia, and though he failed to show his full potential, he did indicate some measure of what he was capable of. In the third Test on January 15th 1904, he scored 102 runs (58 and 44) and took 3 wickets for 94 runs (2-58 and 1-36). Also, in the second innings of the last Test on March 5th, Hirst got his best bowling figures in a Test innings when he took 5 wickets for 48 runs.

Yorkshire held a benefit match for Hirst in the 1904 season, which was against Lancashire at Leeds on August 1st 1904, which raised £3,703 2s 3d. (Maypole tea was then 1s 4d (6.5p) to 1s 8d (8.5p) per lb.; sugar was 2d (0.8p) per lb.; whisky was 4s (20p) per bottle, and admission to the county match at Fartown was 6d (2.5p) or 1s (5p).) It seemed that once again Hirst was doing better with the bat, scoring over 2,000 runs in the season for the first time. He finished the season with 2,257 runs at an average of 53.95, and he still managed to pick up 114 wickets.

Hirst got the highest score of his career at the beginning of the 1905 season; it is also the highest score by a Yorkshire player in a county match. It was against Leicestershire at Leicester on May 18th 1905. Yorkshire were struggling. With 3 wickets down and they only had 22 runs on the board, when Hirst came out and hit the ball all over the field for his 341 runs.

G.H. Hirst's innings at Leicester was a splendid performance. He went in on Friday just before lunch, and at that time Yorkshire had lost 3 wickets for 22 runs. He was the last man out on the Yorkshire side on Saturday, and had then been in seven hours and scored 341 runs. This is the largest innings for or against Yorkshire, the highest score recorded was 318 by Mr. W.G. Grace for Gloucestershire at Cheltenham, so far back as Aug 17-18-1876.

Huddersfield Weekly Examiner
May 27th 1905

The Hirsts' third child, Molly, was born just before the start of the 1906 season on April 29th, and (to the dismay of the other counties) Hirst celebrated the birth in style.

He took 11 wickets for 110 runs (4-47 and 7-70) against Kent at Catford on May 17th; he then took 12 wickets for 66 runs (7-18 and 5-48) against Leicestershire at Leeds on May 21st. He was in form with the bat too, and scored his 1,000th run of the season against Kent at Brammall Lane, Sheffield, on June 25th. Hirst took his 100th wicket of the season in Yorkshire's next match, which was against Essex at Leyton on June 28th.

Hirst kept it up for the rest of the 1906 season. He took 14 wickets for 97 (7-27 and 7-70) against Nottinghamshire at Dewsbury on July 5th. He rounded the season off by scoring 111 and 117 not out and taking 11 wickets for 115 runs (6-70 and 5-45), against Somerset at Bath on August 27th. When the season ended Hirst had scored 2,170 runs and he had taken 203 wickets, and he became the only cricketer to do the 'double double'.

The season took its toll on him, however, and as the 1906 season was drawing to a close he was suffering more and more with a knee injury. It was a struggle for him to pull his boots on, let alone take to the field. He summed it up with these few words:

It gave me gip – after I'd got the runs and the wickets. The feat was a triumph of spirit over matter.

Huddersfield Weekly Examiner
May 15th 1954

The 1907 season started a bit more slowly for Hirst, but he soon got back in the swing again, and at Glossop on July 25th 1907, he and Rhodes bowled Derbyshire out for 44 and 72, with Hirst taking 11 wickets for 44 runs (4-22 and 7-22). Hirst followed that up with 15 wickets for 63 runs (8-25 and 7-38) against Leicestershire at Hull on August 1st, which included his second hat-trick, much to the delight of the press.

Last night Hirst did the hat trick for the second time in his career, hitting the wicket each time, and his first success, curiously enough, was against Leicestershire twelve years ago. To-day he and Rhodes wiped out the remaining six batsmen in thirty-five minutes, the whole innings lasting no more than seventy minutes.

Huddersfield Daily Examiner
August 2nd 1907

Then in the second innings against Middlesex at Brammall Lane, Sheffield, on August 12th, Hirst took 9 wickets in an innings for the first time, taking 9 for 43 runs. Hirst was picked for three Test matches against South Africa in the 1907 season. He only had one good performance, which was in the last Test at the Oval on August 19th, taking 6 wickets for 81 runs (3-39 and 3-42).

At the beginning of the 1908 season Hirst and Haigh bowled out Northamptonshire, at Northampton, for 27 and 15, with Hirst taking 12 wickets for 19 runs (6-12 and 6-7)!

In the first Test against Australia at Edgbaston on May 27th 1909, Hirst showed just what he was capable of, getting his best bowling figures in a Test match, taking 9 wickets for 86 runs (4-28 and 5-58). But that was a one-off and he only took 7 wickets for 252 runs in the next three Tests. He was dropped for the fifth Test at the Oval and he was never picked by England again.

Hirst started the 1910 season by getting his best bowling figures in a county innings. It was against Lancashire at Leeds on May 16th, and he took 9 wickets for 23 runs in the second innings finishing the game with 13 wickets for 78 runs. The rest of the season wasn't so prolific for Hirst, but he still finished top of both the batting and bowling averages for Yorkshire. At this time the family moved to Glebe Street, Marsh, which was a more desirable part of Huddersfield.

Hirst started the 1911 season with a fine all-round performance against Worcestershire, at Worcester on May 22nd, taking 11 wickets for 125 runs (9-41 and 2-84); and he scored a century in Yorkshire's first innings.

Hirst's last exceptional bowling performance for Yorkshire was against Leicestershire at Leeds on June 9th 1913. He took 10 wickets for 48 runs (7-33 and 3-15).

At the beginning of the 1914 season Hirst got 146 against Hampshire at Southampton on May 20th, and he and D. Denton put on 341 runs for the fourth wicket. The papers were more interested with the activities of the Suffragette movement, especially with the arrest of Sylvia Pankhurst, and the raid on the offices of the Women's Social and Political Union, than what was going on in the sports field, and Hirst's feat went virtually unnoticed.

During the Great War, their son, James, joined the West Yorkshire regiment, and the Hirst family had the agonising wait for any news they could get about him. But James was one of the lucky ones and he managed to come through the ordeal.

After the war, Yorkshire mainly used Hirst as a batter, and his last two centuries in county cricket helped Hirst get over a 1,000 runs in the season (1,312) for the last time. The first of them (120) was against Essex at Leyton on June 4th 1919, and the second and the last of his 56 centuries (120) was against Warwickshire at Edgbaston, Birmingham, on June 13th 1919.

Throughout his career Hirst was involved with the club where it all started – Kirkheaton – and they made him the president of the club in 1920. In 1921, when it was proposed that Kirkheaton buy the Bankfield ground, he got the ball rolling with a donation of £10.

Yorkshire had a testimonial for Hirst in the 1921 season, which raised £700. (A Buick 6-cylinder touring car was £676; HP sauce was 11½d (4.75p) per bottle, and Bournville cocoa was 9d (4p) per ¼ lb. tin.) At the end of the 1921 season Hirst retired, and he is still second in the list of leading wicket-takers for Yorkshire.

HIRST'S CAREER FIGURES:

Batting

County Runs	32,231
Average	33.93
Centuries	56
Double Centuries	3
Triple Century	1
1,000+ (in a season)	19
2,000+ (in a season)	3
Test Runs	790
Average	22.57

Bowling

County Wickets	2,569
Runs	45,903
Average	17.98
100+ wkt (in a season)	13
200+ wkt (in a season)	1
Test Wickets	59
Runs	1771
Average	30.0

Others

County Catches	518
Double	14
Double Double	1
Test Catches	18

County Championships
1893, 1896, 1898, 1900, 1901, 1902
1905, 1908, 1912, 1919

After his retirement Hirst became the coach at Eton College, and he also helped Yorkshire out. But the question he was asked over and over again about his illustrious career was if he was disappointed about never getting W.G. Grace's wicket, and he just simply replied, 'The old man never took mine.'

Hirst's son James married Alderman Canby's daughter, Irene, at Saint Andrew's, Huddersfield, in October 1923.

Hirst delighted the crowd at the Scarborough Festival on September 11th 1929, when he donned his Yorkshire cap for one last time. It was against the MCC; he only scored 1 run and from his 23 overs he took 0 wickets for 39 runs.

Hirst refused to get drawn into the controversy after the body-line tour of Australia 1932-33, and when a reporter asked Hirst what he thought about the issue Hirst refused to answer. However, when the reporter asked for his opinion off the record, Hirst gave it him. The reporter was true to his word and only printed his answer after the cricketer's death.

'Well then,' he said, 'what I have to say sounds contradictory. It is that all balls are body-line, or alternatively no ball is. If you are going to score off a ball you must get your nose over it, and then its body-line. Next, no ball need be body-line because the batsman is a moveable object.'

Huddersfield Weekly Examiner
May 15th 1954

At the beginning of 1936, Hirst went as coach and umpire on Yorkshire's winter tour of Jamaica.

Hirst never forgot his impoverished upbringing and he would often meet up with one of his old county colleagues that had 'fallen on evil times' and they would sit in Greenhead Park, which is on the outskirts of Huddersfield, and talk about the old times. When his colleague left without a word said, Hirst would always slip a half-crown (12½p) into his pocket.

During the Second World War, Hirst's daughter, Molly, married John C. McDowell at Holy Trinity Parish Church, Huddersfield, in December 1941.

Shortly after the war, Hirst was made an honorary member of Yorkshire Cricket Club after a meeting in 1946.

In 1950 Kirkheaton cricket club offered the public what turned out to be one of the last chances to see Hirst in public. It was on August 26th 1950, when he and Rhodes were invited to lay a commemorative stone for the new Hirst and Rhodes pavilion at Kirkheaton cricket and bowling club. But he had to make it a brief visit because he had just got out of a nursing home the day before; he made a brief speech and finished it off by saying:

I have spent hundreds of hours on the field practising. I used to be on before six at night and, if we could stay, until 9.30 and 10. It is the only way to learn.

Huddersfield Daily Examiner
August 28th 1950

Sadly, his wife, Emma, died at the age of 79 on June 12th 1953, and she was cremated at Lawnswood Crematorium, Leeds, after a service at Holy Trinity Parish Church, Huddersfield, on June 15th.

On March 23rd 1954, Hirst was due to make what would have been his last public appearance. He was due to appear at the Huddersfield Town Hall, when the Huddersfield and District Cricket League paid their tribute to the triumvirate, by presenting the Mayor with three inscribed silver plates. But his health failed him and he had to pull out at the last minute; his son, James, represented him instead.

Just less than twelve months after the death of his wife, George Herbert Hirst died at the age of 82 on May 10th 1954. He was cremated at Lawnswood Crematorium, Leeds, after a short service at Holy Trinity Parish Church, Huddersfield on May 14th.

A subscription fund was set up to honour Hirst by building a memorial clock at the Fartown cricket club; but that was changed to a memorial clock to commemorate the triumvirate of Hirst, Haigh and Rhodes.

When my research was finished I still wasn't happy about not being able to find details of George Herbert's birth, so I went back to look through the national Register of Births for him and I still came up with nothing. Then I noticed that in the 1881 census he was down as the son of Mary Elizabeth and John Berry and this gave me a good idea about where to look next.

I already knew Mary Elizabeth was born before Sarah Maria married James Hirst, and she was baptised as a Woolhouse, so I went back to look for George Herbert in the national Register of Births. This time I was successful and I found the secret that the family had managed to hide for well over a century. I can confirm George Herbert was born on September 7th 1871, at Saint

Mary's, Kirkheaton, but he was registered as the son of Mary Elizabeth, and he was registered under the name of George Herbert Woolhouse.

Schofield Haigh

Schofield Haigh was born at Church Terrace, Berry Brow, Huddersfield, on March 19th 1871. He was the youngest child of John S., and Elizabeth Haigh (née Jepson); his father was a cloth presser. He had three brothers: Allen Schofield, born in 1856; Jepson, born in 1860; and Tom, born in 1862. He had two sisters – Elizabeth Ann, born in 1858, and Cara, born in 1869. Although they lived near Saint Paul's Church, Armitage Bridge, they attended the Salem New Connection Chapel at Berry Brow.

Haigh started playing cricket at the Berry Brow cricket club, before moving to the Armitage Bridge cricket club. Haigh's first professional engagement was with the Aberdeenshire cricket club, after Louis Hall recommended him to them in 1891. Because of Haigh's youthful appearance the locals were at first a bit disappointed in Hall's decision, but he soon won them over. Haigh stopped with them until 1894, when he moved to Perth. During his time in Scotland, Haigh was also picked to play in a couple of games for the Yorkshire Second XI.

In the July of 1895, Haigh was picked to play for Scotland against Lancashire. He had a decent match, picking up 7 wickets. This prompted Yorkshire to risk him in their next county match, which was against Derbyshire at Derby on July 8th 1895. He scored 25 runs in the first innings and 36 runs in the second, but he failed to make an impression with the ball. That was his only appearance in a county match that year. But at the end of the season he was picked to play for the Yorkshire Players against the Gentlemen at the Scarborough Festival. This time he equipped himself a bit better and took 7 wickets for 94 runs (5-73 and 2-21).

Haigh's future with Yorkshire was still in doubt at the beginning of the 1896 season, when Haigh was picked to play for the Yorkshire Colts against the Nottingham Colts at Worksop. He got 51 runs and 0 wickets for 32 in the first innings, and a duck and 4 wickets for 37 in the second. Despite this hit and miss performance, Haigh was picked for Yorkshire against Somerset at Taunton on May 11th, but he didn't get the chance to impose himself on the match. Yorkshire gave Haigh another go when they were resting some of their players for the match against Cambridge University on June 4th, and again he failed to show his full worth. He didn't get another chance to prove himself until the end of June.

Haigh was picked to play against Durham at Barnsley on June 22nd 1896, and he was devastating, taking 14 wickets for 50 runs (7-25 and 7-25 from 20 and 20.2 overs). He was then picked for Yorkshire's next match, which was against Australia at Bradford on June 29th. The match didn't start too well for Haigh, who only managed to take 2 wickets for 55 runs in the first innings, and he was also out for a duck. But he redeemed himself in the second innings by taking 8 wickets for 78 runs, and he also scored 13 runs. This was the springboard that his career needed. Haigh was picked for Yorkshire's next county match, which was against Derbyshire at Brammall Lane, Sheffield, on July 2nd. Here he took 12 wickets for 115 runs (6-45 and 6-70). At the end of the season Haigh had managed to pick up 84 wickets for 1289 runs at an average of 15.34, and he was top of the bowling averages for Yorkshire.

Haigh had now established himself as a Yorkshire player, and in the first innings against Surrey at Headingley, Leeds, on July 21st 1897, Haigh took 7 wickets for 17 runs. Then, towards the end of the season against Derbyshire at Bradford on August 19th, he took 11 wickets for 80 runs (6-18 and 5-62), which was in itself a good performance; but it included his first hat-trick in county cricket. The feat was reported in a somewhat subdued manner.

Haigh changed ends and brought about a wonderful alteration in the game. In a couple of overs he sent back Storer, Sugg, Ashcroft, Walker and Gould without a run being scored from him, and as the last three wickets fell to successive balls Haigh had the satisfaction of performing the hat trick.

Huddersfield Daily Examiner
August 20th 1897

Haigh didn't let up in the 1898 season, and against Hampshire at Southampton, which was supposed to start on May 26th, but due to rain the match was started and finished on May 27th, with Haigh taking 14 wickets for 43 runs (8-21 and 6-22). Then, in a low-scoring game against Surrey at Bradford on June 6th, Haigh got the chance to shine with the bat, getting his highest score of the season. His 85 runs helped him and G.H. Hirst set a new Yorkshire record for a ninth wicket stand; the feat looks even more impressive when you notice that they put on 192 runs out of a Yorkshire total of 297 runs (report in the G.H. Hirst chapter). Haigh was then picked for the Players against the Gentlemen, in the second of the matches at Lord's on July 18th. The match was delayed in the honour of W.G. Grace's 50th birthday. Haigh got 2 wickets and scored 21 runs.

But his mind may not have been on the match, because on his return from London he got married to Lillian Beaumont at the Paddock New Connection Chapel, on July 31st 1898.

Haigh was picked by Lord Hawke to tour South Africa in the winter of 1898-99, and his first Test match was at the Old Wanderers' Ground, Johannesburg, on February 14th 1899. He got 5 wickets for 121 runs (3-101 and 2-20). But in his second Test at the Newlands, Cape Town, on April 1st, Haigh showed just what he could do with the ball, taking 9 wickets for 99 runs (3-88 and 6-11). At the end of the tour, Haigh was the top bowler with 107 wickets for 876 runs at an average of 8.18.

Unfortunately for Haigh, the tour was marred by the news that his mother, Elizabeth, had died at the age of 65 on January 11th 1899. But he and Lillian had some good news too; their first child, John Scot, was born on January 23rd.

Haigh struggled with his form in the 1899 season. His long run-up and his bowling action was taking its toll on his body, so at the end of the season he decided to shorten his run-up and remodel his action; but this new bowling action meant he wasn't as quick, so he had to outwit the batters.

His new-style action was unveiled with devastating effect in the 1900 season. He took 9 wickets for 80 runs (3-26 and 6-54) against Derbyshire at Derby on June 25th, but he was overshadowed by his team-mate, W. Rhodes, who took 11 wickets for 77 runs. Haigh also took 13 wickets for 94 runs (6-61 and 7-33) against Middlesex at Headingley, Leeds, on August 13th. At the end of the season he had managed to take over a hundred wickets for the first time (160), and he was second in the Yorkshire averages with an average of 14.82.

His 1901 pre-season training was interrupted by the birth of the Haighs' second child, Lillian, on February 5th.

Haigh had a good start to the 1901 season, and he was at the top of his game when Yorkshire played Nottinghamshire at Trent Bridge, Nottingham, on June 20th. He and Rhodes bowled unchanged and they brought the Nottinghamshire first innings to a close for just 13 runs, Haigh getting 4 wickets for 8 runs. In the return match at Sheffield on July 22nd, Haigh got the first of his four centuries, ending with 159 runs. This was also his highest score.

At the beginning of the 1902 season Haigh took 6 wickets for 27 runs in Yorkshire's match against Somerset at Sheffield on June 16th. Not over-spectacular, but he took the 6 wickets in a devastating second innings spell for just 19 runs, and it also included another hat-trick. This time he got a more enthusiastic write-up:

Haigh finished off the innings in wonderful style. With the score on 105 he got rid of Braund, Lee and Newton with consecutive balls, thus accomplishing the hat trick, and subsequently bowling Lewis and Evans, not a run being scored from him while he dismissed the last five batsmen.

Huddersfield Weekly Examiner
June 21st 1902

Haigh went on to finish the 1902 season in fine style, by taking 11 wickets for 81 runs (7-38 and 4-43) against Worcestershire at Harrogate on August 11th, and he followed it up with 12 wickets for 79 runs (5-39 and 7-40) against Middlesex at Lord's August 21st. These performances helped Haigh to become the top bowler in first class cricket in the 1902 season.

The effort seemed to have taken its toll, and Haigh only managed one notable performance in the 1903 season, which was against Essex at Sheffield on August 17th, taking 8 wickets for 24 runs (5-13 and 3-11). But he still finished with over 100 wickets that season.

Haigh bounced back with both bat and ball in the 1904 season, taking 10 wickets for 49 runs (4-28 and 6-21) against Hampshire at Headingley on June 27th. He scored 138 against Warwickshire at Birmingham on June 30th and he also took 6 wickets for 105 runs (3-59 and 3-45). In the next match he got another century. This time it was 104 against Derbyshire at Sheffield on July 4th, and again he took 6 wickets for 113 runs (5-85 and 1-28). These performances helped Haigh achieve the double of 1,000+ runs (1,031) and 100+ wickets (118) – for the only time in his career.

Haigh only managed a couple of notable performances in the 1905 season, taking 12 wickets for 95 runs (6-36 and 6-59) against Worcestershire at Leeds on May 29th, and 12 wickets for 55 runs (6-34 and 6-21) against Nottinghamshire at Sheffield on June 19th.

Haigh was also picked by England to play against the Australians in the second Test at Lord's on June 15th 1905, and the third Test at Headingley on July 3rd. They both finished as draws, with Haigh only managing to pick up 4 wickets. Despite his England performances, Haigh finished top of the bowlers in first class cricket that season.

With Haigh being the top bowler, it was decided to pick him to go on England's 1905-06 winter tour of South Africa. This time it was a bit of a disaster. England lost the tour four-one, and Haigh spent most of the tour suffering from dysentery. In the five Test matches he only managed to pick up 6 wickets, and 4 of them were in the same match.

When he returned from the tour, Haigh was constantly picking up wickets for Yorkshire. He took 12 wickets for 105 (7-46 and 5-59) against Middlesex at Lord's on June 14th 1906. He was picked for the Players once again, but yet again he failed to reproduce his county form. Despite the lack of big wicket matches, Haigh still finished the season with 174 wickets, which was his highest haul of wickets for Yorkshire.

In the 1907 season Haigh took 9 wickets for 67 runs (5-9 and 4-58) against Essex at Leyton on July 11th, and he followed it up with 13 wickets for 40 runs (6-27 and 7-13) against Warwickshire at Sheffield on July 22nd. Haigh had just enough time to finish the game before his wife gave birth to their third child, Reginald

Erskine, on July 25th. Despite not getting 100+ wickets in the season he was still top of the bowling averages for Yorkshire, with an average of 11.51.

Haigh didn't get any big wicket hauls in the 1908 season, but he was constantly picking them up, and he finished the season with 71 wickets. It must have seemed a disappointing season for Haigh, but he had taken the wickets at an average of 12.11, and he was the top bowler in first class cricket again.

Haigh had a good start to the 1909 season; he took 9 wickets for 77 runs (7-32 and 2-45) against Essex on May 17th. Against the old enemy, Lancashire, in their own backyard at Manchester on May 31st, Haigh got the third of his hat-tricks, and he finished the match with 9 wickets for 36 runs (7-25 and 2-11).

Haigh was picked for the second Test against Australia at Lord's on June 14th 1909, but again he didn't show his true potential and he was dropped.

Haigh didn't let this setback deter him and he soon got back in the swing for Yorkshire, taking 11 wickets for 92 runs (4-48 and 7-43) against Leicestershire at Leicester on July 8th 1909.

Yorkshire declared that the match against Lancashire at Bradford on August 2nd was to be a benefit match for Haigh; it raised £2,071 9s. (Netherwood Bros, automobile engineers in Huddersfield, made the Hotchkiss car, an ideal, quiet, powerful and economical, motor. Models from 16 HP at £440; Indian pale ale was 1s 9d (9p) per dozen half-pint bottles; butter was 1s (5p) per lb.; eggs were 1s (5p) per 20.) In his introduction to the match, Lord Hawke described him as *'a great player; one who is known to smile even in the tightest of corners'*. Haigh had a decent match, taking 6 wickets for 58 runs (3-33 and 3-25), and he was not out in both innings. He finished the season with 120 wickets, and he was the top bowler in first class cricket yet again.

The 1910 season was a poor one for Haigh and Yorkshire, with him only picking up 68 wickets at an average of 20.19.

Sadly his father, John Schofield Haigh, died at the age of 78 on January 18th 1911.

Haigh bounced back a bit in the 1911 season. He took 4 wickets for 34 runs (0-15 and 4-19) and he scored 111 runs when Yorkshire beat an All-Indian XI on July 10th. He also took 8 wickets for 24 runs (1-4 and 7-20) against Sussex at Leeds on July 14th. When the season closed he had just missed out on the double, just managing to take 100 wickets in all matches, but only scoring 906 runs. It was another poor season for Yorkshire, and some recriminations started to appear in the papers, but the triumvirate escaped most of them.

The great Huddersfield triumvirate of Hirst, Haigh and Rhodes have rendered exceptional service, but they cannot go on forever.

Huddersfield Weekly Examiner
September 2nd 1911

The criticism lifted Haigh in the 1912 season, and when Yorkshire played Australia at Bradford on June 10th, he took 11 wickets for 36 runs (5-22 and 6-14). He was on form in the county matches too, and in the first innings against Gloucestershire at Leeds on June 12th, he got his best bowling figures in an innings in a county match, taking 9 wickets for 25 runs. He finished the match off by taking 5 wickets for 40 runs in the second innings.

These performances got Haigh's name back on the England team sheet, and England picked him for the last time in the triangular tournament against Australia at Old Trafford on July 29th 1912. His last match was a rain-affected one and it petered out to a draw.

Haigh consistently picked up wickets throughout the 1912 season, and he finished with over 100 wickets for the last time; it was also the last time he finished top of the bowling averages for Yorkshire.

Haigh was struggling with his form in the 1913 season, only managing to take 39 wickets, which was his lowest tally of wickets since his first season, and at the end of the season came the following news:

On Wednesday Schofield Haigh's connection with Yorkshire cricket came to an end. He has accepted the post of coach at Winchester School, and the world of cricket therefore will know him as a player no more. As a sportsman, there is no one more cheery and great-hearted.

Huddersfield Weekly Examiner
September 6th 1913

95

Haigh is still the third in the list of leading wicket-takers for Yorkshire.

HAIGH'S CAREER FIGURES:

Batting
County Runs   11,099
Average   19.00
Centuries   4
1,000+ (in a season)   1
Test Runs   113
Average   7.33

Bowling
County Wickets 1,919
Runs   29,546
Average   15.42
100+ wkt (in a season)   13
Top of first class Aves.   4
Test Wickets   24
Runs   622
Average   25.91

Others
County Catches 276
Double   1
Test Catches   8

County Championships
1896, 1898, 1900, 1901, 1902
1905, 1908, 1912

After his retirement Haigh became the coach at Winchester, and his eldest son, John Scot, was getting the reputation of being a promising sportsman in his own right.

Everything was going well for the Haighs, but with the outbreak of the Great War the country was turned upside down. Like a lot of the young men of the time, John Scot Haigh couldn't wait to come of age so he could go and join up and go on the 'big adventure' in France.

John Scot got his chance to join up, and like a lot of the young adventurers he became a pilot, and he signed for the 'thirty minuters'. As was the case with a lot of his comrades, it was his family who had the nerve-racking wait for the dreaded knock on the door. That knock duly came and they got the telegram, saying their son, RAF 2nd Leut. John Scot Haigh, had been killed in action at Bertangles on August 15th 1918. His death was also reported in the casualty column in the papers.

Killed in Action: Sec. Lt. John Scot Haigh (19) Royal Air Force (pilot) is officially reported killed. He is a son of Schofield Haigh of 174 Taylor Hill Road, Berry Brow, the well-known Yorkshire cricketer. Before the war he was a member of the staff of Messrs. Thomas Hirst and son, wool merchants, of Huddersfield, and was regarded as having a promising business career before him. He played cricket with the Armitage Bridge Club, and also a member of the cricket and football teams of the YMCA.

Huddersfield Daily Examiner
August 19th 1918

John Scot Haigh was buried in Vignacourt Cemetery, France. The news hit the family hard, and the smile was gone from the face of the cheery Yorkshireman, Schofield Haigh.

Just as the family were coming to terms with the tragic news, Schofield himself died at the age of 49, on February 27th 1921. He was buried at Saint Paul's Church, Armitage Bridge, on March 27th. The grave is marked with a marble cross on a stepped plinth.

Wilfred Rhodes

Wilfred Rhodes was born on October 28th 1877, at Moor Top, Kirkheaton, and he was baptised at Kirkheaton Parish Church on December 9th that year. He was the second son of Alfred and Elizabeth Rhodes (née Holliday); his father was a coal miner and they were married on December 26th 1873. His elder brother, Hollin, was born on March 18th 1875.

Little is written about their early life but as was the norm in those days the Rhodes family moved house a few times, either to find work or for a better standard of living. The boys' schooling is a mystery too. There is no record of them at Kirkheaton School, but they might have gone to one of the other schools in the area. After school, Rhodes would either have gone to work with his father in the pit or join his brother on the railways; but it was said his father didn't want him to do any job that would interfere with his cricket, so he might have got Wilfred a job on the pit surface.

Rhodes joined the Kirkheaton cricket club at an early age, and he would practise his bowling at every opportunity. Rhodes learnt that by dipping an old ball in chalk and bowling it against an old barn or shed he could see how the ball would spin. He would also pester the older cricketers for advice on how to spin the ball.

Rhodes was given the opportunity to play for Yorkshire in a trial match against the MCC at Lord's on May 12th 1898. He took the bull by the horns and took 6 for 53 (2 for 29 and 4 for 24). That performance was good enough for Yorkshire to pick Rhodes in their next county match, which was against Somerset, at Bath, on May 16th, and he took 13 for 45 (7 for 24 and 6 for 21). His father's faith in his abilities was amply justified. Rhodes further secured his place in the team by taking 12 wickets for 70 runs (5-46 and 7-24) against Surrey at Bradford on June 6th the same year. Rhodes finished his first season with 141 wickets, which helped Yorkshire reclaim the County Championship.

Everything was on the up for Rhodes, and he got engaged to

Sarah Elizabeth Stancliffe, who was the local grocer's daughter.

The 1899 season started well for Rhodes. He took 15 wickets for 56 runs against Essex at Leyton on May 25th; this included his best bowling figures in an innings in a county match – 9 wickets for 28. He was picked for England and played in the first Test against Australia at Trent Bridge on June 1st, under the captaincy of W.G. Grace, and he finished his first Test match with 7 wickets for 118 runs (4 for 58 and 3 for 60).

Rhodes finished the 1899 season in emphatic style for Yorkshire, taking 11 wickets for 112 runs (3-74 and 8-38) against Nottinghamshire at Trent Bridge, Nottingham, on August 17th. He followed it up at the Scarborough Festival by taking his best bowling figures in an innings for all matches with 9 for 24 against Australia on August 31st, for C.I. Thornton's XI.

Then his world was turned upside down. On September 15th of that year came the tragic news that his brother, Hollin, had fallen from the engine of the train he was stoker on, and he had subsequently died from the injuries he had sustained. An inquest was held into the circumstances of the 24-year-old's death, at the Halifax Royal Infirmary, on September 18th, and Rhodes was called as the first witness to confirm the identity of the body. The jury returned a verdict of accidental death with the recommendation of 'a rail or some provision should be made by the company with a view to prevent as far possible such accidents in the future'. Hollin was buried at Kirkheaton Cemetery, on September 19th 1899.

In the close season, Rhodes married his fiancée, Sarah Elizabeth Stancliffe, as planned, at Kirkheaton Parish Church, on October 11th 1899.

With all the emotional turmoil of 1899 you would have forgiven Rhodes for being a bit subdued at the beginning of the 1900 season, but Rhodes had other plans. He made one of his best starts to a season. He got 11 wickets for 36 runs (4-16 and 7-20) against Worcestershire at Bradford on May 7th 1900; 7 wickets for 72 runs in the first innings in a rain affected match against Derbyshire at Sheffield on May 21st; 8 wickets for 43 runs in the first innings against Lancashire at Bradford on June 11th; and 9 wickets for 78 runs (2-32 and 7-46) against Essex at Layton.

Rhodes took his 100th wicket of the season against Hampshire at Hull on June 21st, and he finished the match with 14 wickets for 66 runs (6-43 and 8-23).

His season just powered on. He got 11 wickets for 77 runs (7-32 and 4-45) against Derbyshire at Derby on June 25th; 7 wickets for 59 runs in the second innings against Sussex at Sheffield on July 9th; 14 wickets for 192 runs (8-72 and 6-120) against Gloucestershire at Bradford on July 23rd; 14 wickets for 68 runs (6-40 and 8-28) against Essex at Harrogate on August 2nd; 13 wickets for 103 runs (6-36 and 7-67) against Gloucestershire at Cheltenham on August 16th. He finished this prolific season for his county with 240 wickets at an average of 12.72, and he had taken 261 wickets in all first class matches. As such he became the first Yorkshire bowler to finish top of the first class bowling list.

The following season was just as prolific for Rhodes with the ball. He got 14 wickets for 141 runs (7-78 and 7-63) against Gloucestershire at Bristol on May 9th 1901; 13 wickets for 96 runs (6-41 and 7-55) against Leicestershire at Leicester on May 30th; 12 wickets for 134 runs (8-53 and 4-81) against Middlesex at Lord's on June 6th; and again he reached the 100 wicket mark on June 21st.

Rhodes kept it up for the rest of the 1901 season, taking 12 wickets for 86 runs (7-20 and 5-66) against Gloucestershire at Hull on July 29th; and 11 wickets for 90 runs (8-55 and 3-35) against Kent at Canterbury on August 22nd. He finished the season with 233 wickets for his county, and he was the top bowler in first class cricket again. He then went on to get his first century (105) for Yorkshire; that was against the MCC at the Scarborough Festival on August 26th.

Rhodes slowed down a bit in the 1902 season and gave only a few notable performances. He took 10 wickets for 56 runs (7-24 and 3-32) against Middlesex at Bradford, on June 9th; 12 wickets for 58 runs (5-22 and 7-36) against Gloucestershire at Leeds on July 21st; and 12 wickets for 54 runs (8-26 and 4-28) against Kent at Catford. At the end of the season he was second in the Yorkshire bowling averages to Schofield Haigh, with 174 wickets at an average of 12.17.

Rhodes was also included in all of England's Test matches,

which were against Australia. Taking 22 wickets for 336 runs (8-26, 6-96, 7-130 and 1-84), with his best performance being 7 wickets for 17 runs in the first innings of the first Test at Edgbaston.

The Rhodeses also celebrated the birth of their daughter, Muriel, at Bog Hall, Kirkheaton, on August 25th 1902.

Rhodes went from strength to strength, and in 1903 season he did the double of 100 wickets (193 at an average of 14.57) and 1,000 runs (1,137 at an average of 27.07) for the first time.

Rhodes was invited on the 1903-04 England tour of Australia. He took 31 wickets at an average of 15.74, and in the second Test at Melbourne on January 1st 1904 he took 15 wickets for 124 runs (7-56 and 8-68).

His career was everything his father had hoped it would be, but on August 4th 1909 the man who had encouraged him all the way to the top of his profession died at the age of 63. In the cricket column a small passage was written in honour of the passing of Alfred Rhodes:

Everyone will sympathise with Wilfred in the cause of his absence from the team. But Rhodes has the satisfaction of knowing that his father, before he was called away, had seen his fondest hopes realised to the full. It is not given to many of us to have our ambitions so amply fulfilled as had the enthusiastic cricketer who from the first dedicated his son to cricket, and laid all his plans with that view. Mr. Rhodes, sen., gave his son every opportunity in his power to learn our great summer game, and would not allow him to engage upon any work which might impede the progress of his son, and one can imagine the deep feelings of the content that must have filled the heart of his father of a cricketer whose name will go down linked with those of the giants of the game. Tomorrow will be laid to rest the remains of one to whom the gratitude not of Rhodes alone, but of all Yorkshiremen and Englishmen, is due.

Huddersfield Daily Examiner
August 6th 1909

Straight after Alfred's funeral at Kirkheaton Cemetery on August 7th, Wilfred had to join England at the Oval for the fifth Test on August 9th, as his father would have wanted; but this time there was no outstanding performance to deaden his sorrow. Rhodes still managed to finish the season with 2,094 runs at an average of 40.26, and 141 wickets at an average of 15.89.

Rhodes went on the 1909-10 winter tour of South Africa with England, but his heart didn't seem to be on the game. He only managed to take 2 wickets and only scored 226 runs.

Rhodes also failed to achieve the double in the 1910 season, which was the first time since the 1903 season.

Rhodes bounced back in the 1911 season, taking 9 wickets for 57 runs (2-41 and 7-16) against Derbyshire at Chesterfield on May 25th. Rhodes got a century in both his innings (128 and 115) against the MCC at Scarborough on August 31st. At the end of the 1911 season Rhodes had managed to do the double again.

Yorkshire also held a benefit match for Rhodes. It was against Lancashire at Brammall Lane, Sheffield, on August 7th 1911, but it did not raise as much as was hoped, so an appeal was made by Lord Hawke:

> *The committee of Yorkshire CCC have issued a circular appeal signed by Lord Hawke and Mr. F.C. Troone with respect to Rhodes's benefit as follows: -*
>
> *'We are desirous of soliciting your hearty co-operation in order to secure a satisfactory benefit for Wilfred Rhodes. The profit on his benefit match retailed only £750 14s 5d, compared to £2,200 1s 4d for George H. Hirst, £1,241 16s 4d for Tunnicliffe, £1,180 15s 4d for David Denton and £925 4s 5d for Schofield Haigh. It will thus be seen that in order to reach £2,000, a sum of between £1,300 and £1,400 must be obtained in subscriptions.*
>
> *'We therefore earnestly appeal to you for your kind support, hoping you will forward a subscription to the fund, and get your friend to do the same. No player ever deserved better recognition, and it is hoped you will assist in this special appeal so as to adequately reward Wilfred Rhodes for the great and loyal service rendered to his county and to England.'*

Huddersfield Weekly Examiner
September 16th 1911

After the appeal went out his benefit fund went up to £2,202 1s. (A dozen bottles of stout cost 1s 6d (7.5p); 10 cigarettes were 3d (1p) and a house would set you back £200.)

On the 1911-12 winter tour of Australia it was his batting that was to the front of Rhodes's game. He scored 463 runs in the five Test matches at an average of 57.8. Rhodes scored the first of his two Test centuries in the fourth Test at Melbourne on February 9th 1912, when he scored 179 in the first innings; it was also his highest Test score. His second century came the following winter against South Africa at Johannesburg.

As war was rearing its ugly head over Europe, the Rhodes family moved to Marsh Grove Road, Marsh, which was a more affluent part of Huddersfield; it was also close to his friend and team-mate, G.H. Hirst.

When the war was over and the country was trying to get back to normality, Rhodes started to lift the spirits of the people the only way he knew how – by scoring runs and taking wickets!

Rhodes started the 1919 season by taking 11 wickets for 52 runs (7-47 and 4-5) against Gloucestershire at Gloucester on May 29th. Then he and Mr. D.C.F. Burton put on a seventh wicket stand of 254 runs against Hampshire at Dewsbury on July 14th. Rhodes finished the top bowler in the first class cricket at the end of the 1919 season.

Rhodes kept it up the following season, and he took 11 wickets for 44 runs (4-20 and 7-24), against Derbyshire at Derby on July 10th 1920. This was nothing too exceptional for Rhodes, but it included his only hat-trick in a county match for Yorkshire – and it got him a few more lines in the papers than his seventh wicket record did.

Derbyshire opened their second innings with Oliver and Morton to the bowling of Waddington and Robinson. Twenty-seven runs were scored in fifty minutes, and then a complete change came over the scene, Rhodes taking the wickets of Oliver, Bees and Cadinan in successive balls. This is the first time that Rhodes has performed the hat trick in his first-class career.

Huddersfield Daily Examiner
July 13th 1920

Rhodes never forgot the place where it all started, though, and when it was proposed that Kirkheaton C & B club buy their ground he put his hand in his pocket and donated £10 to help raise the money.

In the early part of the 1921 season Rhodes got his highest score for Yorkshire – 267 not out – against Leicestershire at Leeds on June 11th. It got the following lines in the press.

Rhodes created a new record for himself, beating his previous highest score in first class cricket. In a stay of a little over five hours he reached the boundary thirty times.

Huddersfield Daily Examiner
July 13th 1921

He also took 7 wickets for 56 runs (3-27 and 4-29).

Rhodes just seemed unstoppable, and at the end of the 1923 season he equalled Hirst's feat of 14 doubles. His performance with the ball against Gloucestershire at Bristol on July 25th got the following acclaim:

Rhodes's bowling was the out standing feature of yesterday's cricket at Bristol. He crowned it by taking his last four wickets in four overs for one run, and all through had the young Gloucestershire batsmen almost at his mercy. It was one of his supreme efforts, and brought him many congratulations.

Huddersfield Daily Examiner
July 26th 1923

Rhodes's mother, Elizabeth, died at the age of 77 on December 31st 1923, and she was interred at Kirkheaton Cemetery, with Alfred and Hollin.

At the end of the 1924 season Rhodes made the double record his own.

His daughter Muriel got married to Thomas Henry Burnley, a bank clerk from Leicester, on October 8th 1924 at the Holy Trinity Church Huddersfield.

Rhodes did the double for the last time in the 1926 season and his best bowling performance came in front of his home crowd at Huddersfield against Somerset on June 2nd, taking 14 wickets for 77 runs (6-29 and 8-48). He got just a few words in the paper.

One of the chief features of the game was the bowling of Rhodes, who today
secured eight wickets for 48 runs, and yesterday took six for 29.

Huddersfield Daily Examiner
June 4th 1926

A testimonial was held for Rhodes in 1927, which raised £1,821 2s
2d. (A three-bed house cost £560; Capstan and Players cigarettes
were 10 for 6d (2.5p) and 20 for 11½d (4.75p); Cadbury's milk
chocolate was 1s (5p) per ½ lb. bar.)

At the end of the 1928 season Rhodes was the top of the
bowlers in first class cricket for the last time.

At the beginning of the 1929 season Rhodes got the acclaim in
the papers by taking 12 wickets for 80 runs (3-41 and 9-39)
against Essex at Leyton, on May 11th.

*Were it not that Wilfred Rhodes is a name that is indelibly stamped upon
the minds of cricketers, the world runs a great risk of receiving some
nickname in view of his wonderful feats year after year. Before he was
Rhodes's age W.G. Grace was known as the 'Grand old man' of the
cricket field; but Rhodes, who must have a considerable steak of radium in
his combination is more likely to be known as 'the Eternal Youth of
Cricket'. On Tuesday at Leyton he had a wicket after his own heart, and
had the batsmen guessing just as he did thirty years ago; Hopkin realised
that desperate measures were called for, and he alone met with any success
against the Kirkheaton wizard.*

Huddersfield Weekly Examiner
May 18th 1929

Rhodes went on his last tour with England in the winter of 1929-
1930, which was in the West Indies. His final Test match was at
Kingston, Jamaica, on April 3rd 1930. He took 2 wickets for 39
runs (1-17 and 1-22) and he was 8 not out and 11 not out.

Not even Rhodes could go on for ever, and at the end of the
1930 season, at the age of 53, he decided to retire from top flight
cricket with Yorkshire; and he still is Yorkshire's top wicket-taker.

RHODES'S CAREER FIGURES:

Batting

County Runs	31,156	
Average	30.10	
Centuries	46	
Double Centuries		2
1,000+ (in a season)		17
Test Runs	2,341	
Average	30.19	
Centuries	2	

Bowling

County Wickets	3,608	
Runs	57,732	
Average	16.00	
100+ wkt (in a season)		22
200+ wkt (in a season)		2
Top of first class Aves.		7
Test Wickets	126	
Runs	3,405	
Average	27.02	

Others

County Catches	586
Double	16
Test Catches	44

He scored over 1,000 runs and took over 100 wickets against Australia

County Championships
1898, 1900,1901, 1902, 1905, 1908, 1912
1919, 1922, 1923, 1924, 1925

After his retirement his love of cricket never diminished. He became the coach at Harrow, and he also helped coach the up-and-coming Yorkshire players. Rhodes still played for Kirkheaton when he could, and in the 1938 season at the age of 60 Rhodes was the top bowler for Kirkheaton, taking 30 wickets with an average of 12.63.

Rhodes was one of the players to be granted honorary life membership of the Yorkshire County Cricket Club, after a meeting in 1946; this was followed with honorary life membership of the MCC in 1949.

Rhodes was often seen with G.H. Hirst in the Huddersfield area and at matches talking about cricket and the old days.

The laying of the commemoration stones of the new Hirst and Rhodes Pavilion at Kirkheaton C & B Club on August 26th 1950 offered one of the last chances to see them together at a public event. But Rhodes had to keep his speech short.

> *Mr. Rhodes cut short his own 'innings', pointing out that he had been a member of the club since the early nineties, began his career there and had always been proud to be associated with the club which, he hoped would have every success in the future.*

Huddersfield Daily Examiner
August 28th 1950

The long days in the field under the sun had taken its toll on Rhodes's sight, and his eyesight finally failed him in 1952. But he still went to the cricket matches, and it was said he could judge a shot by the sound made by the ball hitting the bat.

The Huddersfield and District Cricket League presented a tribute to the triumvirate of three silver plates to the Mayor, for the Corporation silver collection, at the Huddersfield Town Hall on March 23rd 1954. Rhodes was present, along with the sons of G.H. Hirst and S. Haigh.

> *Mr. Rhodes, who spoke at the close, was loudly applauded. He thanked all cricket lovers who had subscribed to the gift and said how very proud he was that his name was on one of the plates.*
>
> *'George Hirst, Schofield Haigh and I were great pals both on and off the field,' he said, 'and we had some very happy times.*
>
> *'But we did not always have it our own way. We had once polished off Essex on the second day, and a cartoon in a London paper had all three of us dressed up and off to Brighton. We played at Brighton and lost the toss, C.B. Fry got a big score of 200, Killick got 200 and Sussex made over 500. In the evening the same cartoonist had all three of us committing suicide.'*

Huddersfield Daily Examiner
March 24th 1954

After the death of Hirst in 1954, Kirkheaton C & B Club made Rhodes the president of the club.

On December 16th 1954, his wife for the last 54 years, Sarah Elizabeth, died, and she was cremated at Lawnswood Crematorium, Leeds, following a service held at Holy Trinity Huddersfield on December 20th 1954.

Shortly after her death he went to live with his daughter and family in Derbyshire. They then moved to Beaumont Road, Canford Cliffs, Bournemouth. But after Muriel's death in 1970, and that of his son-in-law, Thomas, in 1973, Rhodes had to move into a nursing home at Broadstone, Dorset.

He hadn't been at the home long when it was announced that Wilfred Rhodes had passed away at the age of 95, on July 8th 1973. He was cremated in Bournemouth on July 12th, and his ashes were brought back to Yorkshire and placed next to his wife's in the memorial garden at Lawnswood, Leeds.

Printed in the United Kingdom
by Lightning Source UK Ltd.
103178UKS00001B/23

9 781844 013029